Wheelwrights, Watering Cans and Witchell

By Harry Floyd
Wilf Floyd
Oliver Floyd
and Diana Arnold

To my friend Carol

love

Diana x

Published by Legend Publishing, 2000

Copyright® 2000 Diana Arnold

Printed and bound in Great Britain by
Basingstoke Press

ISBN: 0-9538689-0-7

Legend Publishing, Jubilee Cottage,
Old Vyne Lane, West Heath,
Baughurst, Hants. RG26 5LF
01256 851711

Acknowledgements

This book has been over a hundred years in the making.

These are the memories, muses and observations of four members of three generations of a family – my family – the Floyd family. I may have changed my surname on my marriage, but I am a Floyd underneath. The other three contributors were always Floyds – my grandfather Harry, my father Oliver and my uncle Wilf. My father's contribution is small; he died before he could finish his memories of Wendover, but he was the inspiration and encouragement behind my love for writing. He also encouraged me to be curious and inquisitive. I am also grateful to my grandmother, Florence, who never seemed to throw anything away!

This book is dedicated to the memory of my forebears, Harry, Oliver and Wilf and also to the rest of my family, Floyds, Arnolds and Burrows alike, who have encouraged me to put, not pen to paper, but fingers to keyboard!

I hope that future generations of our family and the inhabitants of Wendover and its environs will get as much enjoyment out of reading this book as I have had in putting it all together.

– Diana Arnold, April 2000

For Mike, Gavin and Barbara
and to the memory of Harry, Oliver and Wilf.

Contents

List of plates

Foreword by Diana Arnold

HARRY FLOYD

Chapter 1	My Parents
Chapter 2	Early Memories
Chapter 3	Early School
Chapter 4	Bear and Cross
Chapter 5	Borough and Forrence
Chapter 6	Personalities
Chapter 7	Neddy, Soldier, Foxy and Jacob
Chapter 8	Church Farm
Chapter 9	Animals at Church Farm
Chapter 10	Sticky Knickers and Norfolk Suits
Chapter 11	Seasons at Church Farm
Chapter 12	Fairs and Shows
Chapter 13	The Monastery and Burnt Hands

WILF FLOYD

Chapter 14	Harry Thomas Floyd
Chapter 15	Florence Floyd
Chapter 16	Coachbuilding Between the Wars
Chapter 17	Wendover School
Chapter 18	Social Events in Wendover
Chapter 19	Religious Life and Wendover Church
Chapter 20	Changing Face of Wendover

OLIVER FLOYD

Chapter 21	Along London Road

DIANA ARNOLD

Chapter 22	The Lone Ranger

Appendix 1	*The Floyds of Buckinghamshire*
Appendix 2	*Births, Deaths and Marriages*

List of plates

Cover   Thomas Rayner and Harry Floyd in Wendover High Street. The cottage windows on the extreme right are 29 High Street.

i   Joseph Floyd, Wheelwright, as a young man.

ii   Harry Floyd, with his watering can!

iii   Alice Lavinia Floyd.

iv   The Kings Head, High Street.

v   The Two Brewers.

vi   London Road, also called South St.

vii   Aylesbury Street. The fire station is on the right.

viii   The station bridge.

ix   Florence Floyd, nee Thompson, wife of Harry, mother of Wilf and Oliver and grandmother of Diana.

x   Joseph Floyd.

xi   The funeral of the cub scout, Harry Floyd leading.

xii   Betty, Wilf and Oliver blow bubbles in the back garden of 29 High Street.

xiii   Freeman's at the top of High Street.

xiv   Harry and Florence Floyd in the 1940s.

xv   Oliver and Diana Floyd at a fete in Hale Road.

xvi   Diana in her paddling pool at 27 Hampden Road.

xvii Diana, fourth from left, at her birthday party at 27 Hampden Road.

xviii Diana's birthday party at Twin Wells. Back row l-r: unknown, Joanne Thomas, Diana Floyd, Jenny and Sally. Front l-r: Frances Dunnett, Guy Niblett, Zoe Didsbury and Sharn.

xix   Diana as Telstar, circa 1964.

xx   Barbara Floyd planting a Whitebeam to the memory of her husband, Oliver in March 1980. Mike, Diana and Gavin are far right. Seventh from left is Jack Floyd, next to Cicely Webb, Diana's godmother. The others are friends, relatives and members of the parish council. The tree is flourishing in Witchell.

Foreword

It started with some memoirs written by my grandfather. Then there were some old papers and photographs hoarded over the years in the family home. Both the memoirs and the papers traced some of the family events and recollections of Wendover, but unfortunately my grandfather's writings did not get far beyond his childhood – he started writing them in the 1940s and he died in 1947 (of a kidney disease which subsequently has been found to be hereditary and affecting all four contributors to this book) before he had time to finish them.

Having discovered these treasures, my uncle, Wilf, set about putting it all into an account of one family's involvement with the village. He decided to work backward and forward from the starting point. Backward into some history of the Floyd family, gleaned from public and church records, and forward by recounting some of his personal memories of Wendover in the 1930s.

By 1987 he had put it all together in one volume, which was then photocopied and given to any family member who wished to read it. I was entranced when I received my copy and I believe that these writings may be of interest to the wider family, and perhaps to those interested in Wendover and the area. Since they also include mention of Lacey Green and its association with the Floyd name, it is possible that other branches of the family may one day find it an interesting start point for their own researches.

Wilf died in June 1995 and, having spoken to other members of the family, in particular his son, Michael, and sister, Betty, it was decided that I should retype it and generally make it ready for publication. In 1999 I found Oliver's contribution written shortly before his death in 1979, whilst sorting out my mother's loft prior to her moving house. This then is the result, and I hope you find it as absorbing a read as I first did, and have again since 'taking it over'.

There are five sections to the record:

Section 1   Harry T. Floyd on Wendover and personal events.

Section 2   Wilfred J. Floyd on Wendover and family connections

Section 3   Oliver R.T. Floyd's recollections of Wendover

Section 4   More recent memories of Diana Arnold (nee Floyd)

Section 5   Some history of the Floyd family from the 16th Century

Harry Floyd

Chapter 1

My Parents

This autobiography, or whatever you prefer to call it, starts in the year 1888. Not because that was the year in which I was born, but because that year saw a great change in the lives of two people, a man and his wife who, with one small child – a little girl of about 18 months – were trying to make a living as innkeepers at *The Bell,* Princes Risborough. The man at the same time was working at his trade as a wheelwright with a man named Benyon, who ran a small country wheelwright's business opposite *The Bell.*

These people were my father, Joseph Floyd, my mother, Elizabeth Anne, nee Rayner, and my baby sister, Alice Lavinia. My father was the eldest son of William Floyd, of Tingewick Wood Farm near Buckingham, and was born, I believe, near Stokenchurch, while my mother was the daughter of Thomas and Lavinia Rayner, of Ellesborough.

It was early in the year 1888 when events took a turn for the worst and my parents decided to try their fortune in another district.

Thus it was that my father heard of an old blacksmith's shop being vacant in the small town of Wendover and at once decided to try his luck by setting up in business as a wheelwright on his own account. So on May 13th 1888 the keys of the old blacksmith's shop in High Street, which I believe had been run for generations by the Carter family (now T. Carter & Sons Automobile Engineers on the opposite side of the street) came into my father's possession and the business of Joseph Floyd, Wheelwright and Coachbuilder came into being. I have heard many tales of the hard struggle my father had in those early days, of the jealousies of other wheelwrights in the surrounding district and the prejudices of certain farmers whose names I prefer not to mention.

The two old cottages beside the shop (how on earth people ever managed to live in them has often puzzled me) were to be made into one single cottage so for the time being my parents lived in Aylesbury Road in the house now occupied by Matthews & Son as a Bakers Shop. My father had one helper, a lad by the name of Harry Goodchild, who had known him at Princes Risborough and had decided to come to Wendover soon after my father settled here. This lad, now a very well known man in Wendover, lived with my parents.

I do not know just how long my parents lived in Aylesbury Road, but do not think it was many weeks. The business progressed and the petty prejudices and jealousies were gradually lived down, and people began to see that my father was a first-class tradesman. It was, however, still very heavy going as the old ledgers still in my possession will show, but it there ever was a man who could fight an uphill fight, it was Joseph Floyd. I only wish I had the same dogged determination and ability to "come up smiling" in the face of adversity.

It was in such conditions that at 6am on 30th June 1892 I was born. That dearly loved personality Dr E.G. Woollerton brought me into the light of day on that brilliant June morning and, unfortunately, many were the times that he had to be called to the house to attend to me in later years.

My sister was now just on six years old, her birthday being July 30th, tall for her age and, as her photograph shows, a nice-looking child with a happy smile. Stories of her delight at having a baby brother have often be told to me; her only disappointment appears to be due to the fact that "I'd got no sense". How I wish I had known that little sister of mine, but it was not to be.

September 1st 1892 was a great day for the little town of Wendover. Up to that time the mode of travel to London was either by train from Tring which meant a journey by road of roughly seven miles to the east, or from Princes Risborough about the same distance to the west, or to travel by coach all the way. The coach, I believe, used to start from the Red Lion and run to Holborn and was driven by Robert Seeley, who used to live at *The Two Brewers* and whose daughter, Mrs A How, still lives in Wendover. I can just remember Robert Seeley, a fairly big man, heavily built of the old fashioned "John Bull" type.

For the past few years the Metropolitan Railway had been forging ahead, pushing its way down from London towards Aylesbury and onto Verney Junction, not far from the Claydons where it linked up with the London & North Western (now the L.M.S.) Railway.

I have heard many stories of the building of the railway through Wendover, of the "steam navvies" or excavators digging the deep cutting just on the London side of the Station Bridge – which, by the way, is said to be the deepest cutting on the whole of the line, and of how the railway company wanted to build its engine and carriage works here but could not get permission from the Lord of the Manor.

At last the great day came, September 1st 1892: the day of the formal opening of the railway. It must have been a day of outstanding importance to the people of Wendover. The meadow, now built upon and cut by two roads, Forrest Close and Coombe Avenue, was known then as Marshallsays' Meadow, due to the fact that it belonged to the land farmed by Mr Edwin Marshallsay who lived at Lime Tree House, then a farm, was the scene of a big public tea and sports to mark the occasion. I believe that a procession was formed by the children of Wendover Schools and, headed by a band, marched to the meadow.

My sister was amongst those children; she had a new frock and new boots for the occasion as was the practice of those days, but alas that was the only time she wore them. A cold caught at those celebrations turned to bad chest trouble which was called bronchitis and after a short illness she died on September 24th 1892.

No doubt, had all this happened in these days of medical enlightenment it would have been called pneumonia and with the new advance treatment she would have at least had a chance of living. Instead of which, my parents' joy at my birth was suddenly overshadowed by the death of the elder child.

The opening of the railway made many changes in the life of, not only the Wendover people themselves, but to those living in the surrounding districts. Up to this time, goods of all kinds were carried to and from Wendover either by the great road wagons or by barges on the Grand Junction Canal. Wendover still has its links with those days, the most outstanding of which is of course the old canal wharf, now in ruins. Miss Lilian Barber is the daughter of the last wharfinger, the late Martin Barber. Another link is the Fantham family whose late head, Joseph Fantham, was a bargee who settled at the "Pack Horse" public house, which in the days when the canal was in full use was the public house most frequented by the barge dwellers.

The railway altered all this, although even in my days I remember the road wagons owned by Mr Edwin Marshallsay who, besides begin a farmer was also a hay dealer and had a siding on the Grand Junction Canal at Paddington Wharf. These wagons used to travel to London loaded with hay and return with any merchandise which one or other of the trades people needed. This did not last long after the arrival of the railway and Mr Alfred Payne was the first person to be official agent for delivery of goods brought by rail, as well as having a coal siding in the railway goods yard. I can just remember being taken for a short ride on a trolley built by my father for Mr Payne on its initial run. I believe my ride was as far as the Baptist Chapel. This trolley was built especially for the delivery of goods and coal and caused something of a sensation, painted bright red and lined with blue and yellow and its front board written in gold.

This trolley by the way was in continuous use for more than forty years, a truly great proof of the excellent workmanship of my father.

My earliest recollections of the railways personnel are of Mr George Ratcliffe (now Station Master at Gt. Missenden), "Teddy" Howlett and

George Bishop, usually known as Teddy the porter and George the porter, while soon afterwards Thomas Swain, a signal minder, and Walter Parsons, a plate layer, came into my field of knowledge.

In those days and for years afterwards the fare to London was about 3s 4d return and 7d return to Aylesbury. In later years, just before the Great War one could join an excursion train and travel to the South Coast for about 4s 6d and regularly every Thursday a half day ticket to London, commencing on the 12.55pm train, cost 2s 6d.

Chapter 2

Early memories

Although I find it somewhat difficult to remember many things which happened during my early manhood, I have always been able to remember certain outstanding events which happened during my earliest years, so much so that it has often been my lot to be contradicted when I have said that I could remember this or that event. The picture of High Street as it was then is also firmly fixed in my memory.

One of the events which caused something of a depression among the inhabitants was the death of General Philip Smith, the well-liked Lord of the Manor, on November 1st 1894. Of course his death meant nothing to me but I can remember being taken to the churchyard to see the funeral. The body was borne by eight guardsmen in their scarlet tunics and bearskins. I can see that scene now in my mind's eye. Also I remember seeing them march back to the railway station. This funeral made such a mark on my mind that for a long time one of my favourite games was to carry a furry toy animal called *Monkey* round the room on my shoulder and solemnly "bury" him under the old fashioned sofa cushion. This was known as *Generaling the monkey*.

About this time the Wendover Drum and Fife Band was in full swing. It was under the leadership of the late Mr Charles Freeman. What I remember most about this is that Harry Goodchild was a member of the band and played a flute. On winter evenings he would sit by the fire and play while I duly accompanied him by beating a tea tray with a stick on which was tied a ball of cloth. I was told in later years that noise was my primary object, time being quite a secondary matter. Another thing which stands out clearly is being taken to see the reservoir frozen over and people having rides in a chair which was pushed from one bank to the other by a skater.

Dobbins Lane in those days was a mere cart track, with hedges and big trees on either side, which led to Cold Comfort and the fields which are now built on and form Chiltern Road, Perry Street and what is now known as the residential part of Dobbins Lane. A footpath cut across the land from the station and entered Windmill Meadow, then known as Adam's Meadow, near the top corner of the tennis courts and went straight across the meadow to Mill Path. The present path was made at the time of the making of the present hard road, the correct name of which is Albert Avenue.

At the corner of Dobbins Lane stood a fair-sized grocer's shop, owned by Mr F. W. Blake. The same building still stands and is still a grocer's shop but is vastly different to the original. The old baker's shop, now owned by

Harry Thomson, has not been altered one bit and many are the times that I have gone to see the bread being drawn from the oven and to receive a piece of dough made into the shape of a very small cottage loaf and baked with the real loaves. I believe we used to pay a halfpenny for these, quite a fair sum of money for a child in those days but with a piece of farm butter on them and eaten hot they were delicious.

The house now occupied by Mr H G Landon was then a harness maker's shop and was kept by a old gentleman named George Mead. It had a large shop window, consisting of six very big panes of glass, which was always full of bright brass harness decorations and coloured whip cord, and a large picture of a carriage and horses which advertised somebody's stable requisites.

Mr Mead was an enthusiastic gardener and owned an apple orchard. He used to store apples at the back of the shop behind a large rocking horse which was always loaded with harness and which was the envy of all the small boys. This combination has always had one effect upon me, it is this: whenever I hear the name of Mead no matter where I may be, I instantly seem to sense the smell of a mixture of apples, cobblers wax and Stockholm Tar. Mr Mead was a queer but good hearted old man; one joke against him was that his reply to a customer who complained about some sewing that he had done was: "Young lad, remember, long stitches wear long". I have spent many very interested moments watching him busily repairing harness or looking at that rocking horse and imagining that I was riding it. I have cause to remember that shop window, for my ball went clean through one of the bottom panes and the poor old man was too angry to give it back to me.

Standing next to this harness-maker's shop was the old blacksmith's shop; by that time it was turned into a wheelwrights establishment with a board over the doors bearing the name of Joseph Floyd. Traces of this old shop can still be seen, for instance the stone walls both facing the street and parting the premises from Mr Landon's are remains of the building, while the strips of wood built into the end wall of my cottage were put there on purpose to put nails in for hanging tools on. The concrete flooring at the rear of the cottage is part of the old paint shop floor. I can just remember my father having a pet jackdaw. This bird got so tame that it was decided to let it out to flutter about, its wings being secured so as to prevent its escape, but like the Jackdaw of Reims, it liked pretty things and promptly ate some pieces of brightly-coloured paint skins. Consequence: R.I.P.

There was no yard attached to the shop so it was a common thing to have one or two heavy farm carts or a wagon stood out in the front, leaving just enough room for pedestrians to pass, not that there were many pedestrians

Wheelwrights, Watering Cans and Witchell

after dark compared with the present day. I'm afraid these happenings would be frowned upon very severely by the present day authorities, but I've been told that the policeman of that time (there was only one) used to arrange for the carts to be turned facing the wind and tipped up so that he could stand in it and so be out of the wind. That policeman was Sergeant Neil, father of the present Superintendent Neil.

As I have said before, there was no yard close to the shops so my father rented one very near by.

Before my time the house now used as the Post Office had been a farm house, consequently the ground behind it was the farm yard. In this yard stood several buildings, one of which was used as a timber shed, complete with a saw pit. It was in this yard that the tyre fires were built and it was here in 1900 that a disastrous fire occurred. A large rick of faggots stood near to where the fires were made and about six o'clock in the evening, after one of these tyre fires, this rick was seen to be on fire. A gentle breeze was blowing towards the brewery buildings and before it could be stopped some of the lower buildings, comprising chiefly of pig sties were well alight. A number of pigs were destroyed and a good deal of my father's rough timber.

Water had to be pumped by the old manual fire engine from lower Witchell pond and after the fire was under control the firemen tried their hardest to "accidentally" knock the policeman's helmet off with water. I can't say whether they succeeded or not.

There must have been some kind of farming activities still going on in the yard although I cannot remember what they were, but I do remember seeing a traction engine with threshing tackle being taken down there on several occasions.

What makes me remember this is the fact that the driver had to let the chimney of his engine down to get under the archway at the gate.

Mention of the brewery buildings reminds me to say that the Kings Head yard was the site of Hollands Brewery up to the time of the Great War.

Chapter 3

Early School

The death of my sister, as related in the first chapter, caused my dear mother to lavish extreme care upon me, so much so that I have thought many times since that this coddling and wrapping up caused me to grow up somewhat of a weakling, but who am I to judge that?

As it was, I was rarely allowed out to play after tea time except on summer days, consequently I had few friends. My earliest friends were the How family next door, but my special pal was Bert Landon. His people moved from Aylesbury to the shop where he still carries on business and I can remember quite clearly to this very day my first meeting with him. I can see him now in a little overall pinafore pulling a small tin engine on a string in London Road, sliding his feet and making a hissing sound to represent steam. From then onwards we were almost inseparable, right up to the time that we both joined the army. It sounds strange nowadays to talk of playing on the street but traffic was scarce and one of our great delights was playing in the sand and dust which, in dry weather, laid thickly on the old fashioned flint made roads before Mr Macadam hit on the plan of using granite and tar.

Bert and I were both three years old when our first meeting took place. Our pranks and adventures in the years that followed could fill many books.

As school days approached he went to the Infants School, but owing to my mother's fear for my welfare I was sent to a private school kept by a Miss Bertha Jefferay in the house now occupied by Mr G H C Daniels, Newsagent.

In those days this was a small, single-fronted harness-maker's shop kept by old Mr Jefferay, a tall man with a white beard. The adjoining yard was a farm yard with large oak-beamed barns and stables run by Mr Jefferay's two sons.

Mention of the old buildings recalls the fact that in 1936 I assisted Mr Fred Slade in the demolition of the stable and between the foundation bricks by the doorway I found a William and Mary penny dated 1694. I still have this coin. I can remember those lessons in that little back room; the spelling books, the little Bibles and even the jam jar full of water behind the floor with which we had to wash our slates. The other members of that school included the Sears and the Billington families. One prize I had there was a book *Jack the Giant Killer*. But what I won it for I doubt if even Miss Jefferay knew.

At the age of between eight and nine I went to Wendover School and was

Wheelwrights, Watering Cans and Witchell

put into Standard III under a teacher named Miss Vizer, a tall dark girl with a fiery temper. The Headmaster was Mr John George Bushell, known to the boys as 'Old Four Pecks', a hard master at times but a thoroughly good teacher.

How different are the ways and methods of people nowadays from what they used to be, even in my early days. Vine Tree Farm, now Hibberds Garage, was then really a farm, it was kept by a man named John Field Archer and later by Mr Joseph Holland, father of Mr J S Holland.

Two men who I knew very well used to work on that farm. They were James and George Dancer. James was a tall, strong, raw-boned type of man, while George was a short, round cheery-faced man with a beard. Both lived in London Road and every morning at 4.30am in summer and 5am in winter they could be heard walking down to the farm loudly discussing the weather. They fed and groomed their horses and could then be heard coming home to breakfast in readiness to start work at six.

I can remember these horses, their coats shining like silk and tails and manes neatly plaited or tied with coloured braid. The men could be seen again at night going to "rack up" as it was called; they thought the world of their horses.

Mr Holland also owned the Water Mill behind the School. Many times have I been there to watch the miller, a Mr Honour, at his work. It was one of my mother's delights to tell how I came home one day after having being weighed on the mill scales to tell her that I weighed "Two Ton Two", meaning, of course, two stone two pounds.

I was also a frequent visitor to the old windmill. I can remember the sails and the fantail quite well and have been to the top on several occasions.

My father used to fit new wooden cogs or "re-gear" as it was called, one of the main wheels which drove the grinding stones.

The shops in High Street have been altered a great deal. The draper's shop known as Freeman and Sons was really kept by old Mr Freeman with the assistance of his family. That part of the shop nearest to Carter's Garage (then a blacksmith's shop) was a place where I believe Mr Freeman used to keep his trap. I'm not quite sure what kind of a place it was inside, but I can remember two large doors opening out into the part that was afterwards converted into the Gents Outfitter's department. Part of the drapery department was also used as the Post Office. I have earned many sixpences from that Post Office in later years by acting as auxiliary Telegraph boy. I used to be paid according to the distance travelled, such as 9d for a journey to either Scrubwood or Weston Turville, 6d for Wendover Dean, The Hale or

17

Halton, 4d for Bacombe Warren or "Lower Bacombe" as it was then known, World's End or Wellwick, 2d in Wendover itself, but I'm getting ahead of my story.

To return to the shop itself, Mr Bert Freeman, who was a chemist and therefore attended to that part of the business, was also a photographer. I well remember being taken there to be photographed when I was about four or five years old. This picture shows me as a very weak-looking little boy holding a water can. This was very much against my dear mother's wish, but that is all I would do. A hoop, a pistol, a kite and various other toys were tried, but all to no avail, it was the water can or nothing. The draper's shop on the opposite side of the street was then a plain, double-fronted place kept by a Mr Edwin King and his daughters.

The part of the shop nearest to the present Post Office was then a small cottage occupied by Mr John Philbey, a very small man with a very large wife; his daughter Mrs Pearce, still lives in Wendover, in Castle Park. Mr Philbey was a postman and a tailor, he was also an organ blower at the church. The characteristic of this inoffensive little man was that he was rarely seen to actually walk, his gait was something between a walk and a trot. The front door of this cottage was reached by three nicely-built brick steps which were kept scrupulously clean and reddled. Many were the boyish larks played on these steps to the great annoyance to Mrs Philbey.

The greengrocer's shop kept by Mr George Brackley was then a private house occupied by a Miss Edith Senior, a member of a very old Wendover family which has now become almost extinct. Many years ago this house was the Post Office. Proof of this can still be seen on the wall over the present door and windows. On wet days the place can still be seen where a panel with POST OFFICE was painted on the bricks.

The butcher's shop near to Brackley's was kept by a man named Fred Caudrey, no relation to the Caudrey's now in Wendover, and working for him was a boy named Albert Goodson, who in later years ran a business of his own in Pound Street where he still resides, but the shop has closed down long since. William Smith and Sons, who still have the butcher's shop, Brackley's, came to Wendover from Aylesbury, taking over a butcher's business previously owned by Mr Alan Juson, an old Wendoverian. This shop was at the house now occupied by Mr Fred Hubbard, and was done away with when Caudrey left Wendover and Smith moved into his premises. In those days the shop now used by Arnold Thorne the hairdresser was a grocer's shop run by Mr Pearce, the forerunner of Pearce Bros, now Essex and Son in High Street, this establishment then being occupied by a Mr Paley who, with his family, went to try his fortune in Canada. Of course,

Wheelwrights, Watering Cans and Witchell

Spittles Fish Shop is quite new; these premises were used by Mr E J Sharpe as a shop for cycle repairs. The Drug Stores is also very new. This was a private house, later used as a Bank by the Union of London and Smith's Bank until the building of a new bank on the site of the Pear Tree Cottage garden. "Churchills Cafe" was a small-fronted jewellers shop owned by Mr E J Sharpe and what is now Stocks' jewellers shop was a private house until very recently. The boot shop was a small shop owned by a Mr Foster and later enlarged for a Mr T Harding.

The Red Lion Hotel was quite a different looking place, plain and unattractive but a centre where the business people would meet. Another house that used to be a shop is Archway Cottage, Aylesbury Street. This was a seedsman's establishment run by a tall old man with a beard, Mr Daniel Moore, while the house known now as Chandlers House with its adjoining yard was a Builders house and yard occupied by Mr John Lacey Eldridge who, by the way, married my grandmother's sister as his third wife.

Of course other shops have both been altered and come into being, for instance Southerns and Son was a baker's shop. Deerings was a cottage and the side of Caudreys Cycle shop and Egglestons was a blacksmith's as was also Gardeners Garage, while Billingtons Stores was built for the Salvation Army and was called "The Barrack". Neither of the ladies hairdressers or Saunder's butcher's shop was in being, but in later years a Miss Birdie West, afterwards Mrs Jack Pearce, opened a gents' hairdressers next door to Eggletons shop.

Chapter 4

Bear and Cross

During my early days I always claimed to have two homes, Wendover and Kimble. Naturally Wendover meant more to me, but the very happiest days of my life are centred around Great and Little Kimble. When I was born my grandparents kept the *Bear and Cross*, now altered out of all recognition and called *The Bernard Arms*. It is situated just on top of the hill, close to Great Kimble church and in those days was a general grocers and butchers shop as well as being a public house. In later years the butchery side was dropped but the general shop was kept going.

In the September following my birth my grandparents moved to Church Farm, close to that dear little church at Little Kimble. But before going any further I must relate a few incidents that happened at the *Bear and Cross*, as told to me on many occasions.

Of course the old inn had many visitors and boarders, among the latter was a very outstanding figure in the person of a certain gentleman name Carl Adolph Rittner, well over six foot tall and weighing under ten stone, with a mixture of about six different countries in his blood. He must have been an outstanding figure indeed.

This gentleman came to England with the famous show, Barnum and Baileys Wild West Show of which he was a Ringmaster. I cannot remember this gentleman but I knew Mrs Rittner very well. She owned a most beautiful husky dog named Jukas of which I was very fond. Mr Rittner was a first-class if somewhat wild horseman. It is on record that he once raced the train from Princes Risborough to Kimble on a thoroughbred mare, which he called Wild West, owned by my grandfather and later owned by Dr E G Woollerton.

I recall the story of how my sister was nearly killed by being struck on the forehead by a heavy lump of iron on the end of the old pump handle, this can still be seen at the rear of the premises. It appears that she ran past the pump just as an old man named Don Beckett was swinging the handle. Another story of one named "Squint" Rogers who, not being tall enough to look properly into the old fashioned brick oven, brought a ladder into the kitchen to assist him. On another occasion he cleaned my grandfather's boots with gas tar "to keep the wet out".

Another outstanding event which was well known throughout the whole district and which brought many visitors to the *Bear and Cross* was when my grandfather set himself out to see just how heavy he could fatten a pig up to. He made it known that he would fatten a certain pig up so that it would weigh half a ton. As the time went on more and more people went to Kimble to take a look at the pig whose fame was fast spreading. People used to form parties as far away as Oxford and make a day's outing with a pleasure brake and a pair of horses, travelling to Kimble to see the famous pig. This poor pig got so fat that its legs would not support its great body while it ate. In consequence my father made blocks of wood and fixed them to support the pig during its meals. I have been laughed at and contradicted on many occasions when relating the above facts, but it is only about three years ago since a man died who actually helped to feed the pig. He was Mr Green, father of Jack Green, landlord of the *White Swan*.

My grandfather never obtained his objective of half a ton, the poor pig got to within a very few pounds of the aimed at weight but then began to show signs of failing health.

The favourite pastime of the sportsmen of the district was holding a pigeon shoot, either clay or live birds, and this was just what my grandfather loved, for he was recognised as a first-class shot. He therefore hit on the idea of holding a pigeon shoot in the meadow behind the *Bear and Cross* with the fat pig as the prize. The appointed day arrived and everything was in readiness, most of the leading sportsmen were present. The sweepstakes were paid up and the first shot was ready to be fired when a very well-known gentleman of that time, named Major Jenney of Clotney Dean, called attention to the fact that my grandfather had not entered the contest himself. This caused some argument as everyone wanted to see him shoot. The consequence was that after some discussion my grandfather duly paid his entrance fee and took his turn, and in the end he won the shoot, the sweepstake and the pig.

This was the end of the poor pig, for very soon after this it was killed. To finish the anecdote I must add that when the pig was killed an old man whom I knew very well, named Ben Buckingham, said he would very much like just one pork chop off the carcass. My grandfather gravely cut a pork chop, cutting it right through and rather thick. The story goes that this chop weighed just on 7lbs, but it was almost useless being nearly all fat. I cannot vouch for the part of the story relating to the weight of the pork chop, but I have heard it told and laughed about by several old Kimble people.

Another tale of the *Bear and Cross* days that my grandfather was never tired of telling was of a man calling late one night asking to be put up for the night and stabling for his horse.

My grandfather took a look at the horse, which was harnessed to a spring cart. The animal was in a half-starved condition and looked tired out. The cart with its contents was put into the cart shed and the horse put into the stable where it immediately started to eat the bedding on the floor.

In the morning my grandfather took another look at the horse and cart with its load, which turned out to be books. He was always noted for his impulsive actions and this occasion was no exception. The consequence was that the man walked away, my grandfather having bought the complete outfit. The horse recovered and became a great favourite, for it had once belonged to a circus and the tricks that it could do had been told to my grandfather by its late owner. One trick was to rear up on its hind legs when one rein was shaken in a certain way. Thus it was, that when an old woman for whom my grandfather had a great dislike once asked him for a ride home from Aylesbury he replied, "Oh yes, you can ride if you can get up in the cart." "Oh I can get up all right" replied the woman, but just then the particular rein was shaken and up went Showman (for that is what the horse was called) on his hind legs. Away scrambled the old woman, vowing that she would never ride with such a dangerous horse.

My grandfather was always a lover of horses and I can see him now in my mind's eye, with his iron-grey hair worn rather long as was the fashion, a beard and moustache neatly trimmed and a bowler hat tilted to one side, driving along in a spring cart drawn by a horse with well brushed coat travelling at a good swinging pace. In later years this was replaced by a much slower type, his last horse was an old white pony, which used to toddle along slowly, but it received the same kind attention as the earlier and more dashing animals had done.

As I have stated before, impulsiveness was an outstanding trait in grandfather's character. So it was that one day he returned to the *Bear and Cross* and announced to my astonished grandmother, "Mother we are leaving here, I've taken Church Farm". She was always very much against the change, but Michaelmas 1892 saw them moving into their new home having parted with the old inn and shop to a man named Frank Durling. There are very few people in my life that I can truly say that I really disliked, but Frank Durling was one of them. A man who had left gentleman's service as a coachman on purpose to take a public house. He was cunning and altogether dislikable. My grandfather also disliked him intensely and whenever the two chanced to meet there was always sure to be a steady stream of remarks that were usually too pointed to be called sarcasm.

I knew quite a lot of the old Kimble people who were either customers at the little shop or regular users of the *Bear and Cross* as a public house. It was one of the chain of houses belonging to the then famous brewery owned by Wellers of Amersham. The firm went into voluntary liquidation soon after

Wheelwrights, Watering Cans and Witchell

the Great War and was bought up by Benskins of Watford.

From these old people I heard many stories of the days when my grandfather kept the old inn, in fact it used to seem to me that they based many of the memories from, to use their own term, "them good old days when Tom Rayner and his missus kept the *Bear and Cross*".

Running along on the opposite side of the road to this old pub is a wall. This wall marks the boundary of the Chequers Estate. This ancient estate, now national property, was in those days and for many years later a far more beautiful place than it is now. Water flowed from the side of one part of the high ground and used to run in a big wide stream down through the Church Farm meadows. But for some reason or other it is now only a slight trickle which forms a slow muddy and narrow kind of brook. This beautiful stream started in a small gorge, then over a water wheel which pumped water to Chequers Court and then widened out into a kind of lake on the side of which was a boat house with boats moored inside for the use of the owners of the Estate.

To get a really beautiful picture of all this, one had to turn in at the pretty little lodge which stood just at the top of Gt. Kimble hill, walk along the coach drive (this drive by the way was the Kimble or West Approach to Chequers Court) and then turn abruptly into the trees, walk a few paces and there before you was a most wonderful sight. There you stood under a great tree on a somewhat narrow path which ended abruptly, an almost straight drop down in front of you, looking down a little wooded gorge with its stream opening out into a miniature lake with the green meadows in the near distance. This beauty spot was know as "The Peep". Under the big tree, beneath which you stood to look at this, was a wooden seat and it was said that to see the view properly one must stand on the seat facing the tree, then bend down and look between ones legs. I have done this many times and I have seen others do it. Of course, looked at this way it did look nice, but I have an idea that the whole thing was a gag, for as soon as you saw this view upside down you became aware of the sheer drop which was quite close and from that angle seemed to be magnified, with the result that most people instantly became very giddy and asked to be helped off the seat, to the great amusement of the others who were watching.

I doubt very much if there are many people now living in Kimble who know of this old spot, for it is only about a year ago that I asked a youngish man when I was at Kimble one day if one was allowed to go there now and he vowed that he had never heard of it.

Another beauty spot close by was Kimble Warren, a deep valley, thickly wooded with box trees on each side and at the "deep" end. It was I suppose more of a pocket in the hill rather than a valley for it can only be entered at one end. In the middle of this place stood a keeper's cottage, now demolished, an old timber and wattle place with thatched roof. In the summer roses and honeysuckle fought with every other kind of climbing flower for room to cling to this little cottage and the colours with the dark box background and the bright grass all round made the whole place look like a page from a child's picture book.

Like "The Peep", the Lake and the boathouse, this beautiful spot has been allowed to pass into a state of overgrown wilderness. Kimble Warren is now known at "Happy Valley", though why the "Happy" I can't imagine.

Chapter 5

Borough and Forrence

Before going on to more anecdotes about Kimble I must return to further details as well as memories of Wendover. Since the Air Force personnel from Halton Camp have lived around these parts, Wendover is nearly always spoken of as a village, but in reality it is and always has been a town. Wendover was a town with its own market long before Aylesbury became a place of any importance at all.

It was also divided into two parts, the Borough and the Forrence or "Foreigns" as it was more often called, and consequently was then represented by two members of parliament up to the date when the new franchise came into being. Wendover was what was known as a "Rotten" Borough and at one time was represented in parliament by that great champion of democracy, John Hampden.

The old Borough boundaries have been pointed out to me as follows: Aylesbury St, just below the present Fire Station, Tring Road, Mr Fred Slade's cottage, Pound St, Lime Tree House and London Road, or to give its correct name, South Street, somewhere near the end of the Gospel Hall.

The "Foreigns" were Wendover Dean, Scrubwood and The Lee and Swan Bottom districts and those who lived in these places were "Foreigners". In my school days we used to have prayers just before the close of the day's lessons and in the winter it was a recognised thing for Mr Bushell to call out "Foreigners may go" just before these prayers commenced. This was made use of on many occasions by other children for dodging prayers. Sometime during the afternoon a hand would go up with a "Please Sir can I go with the Foreigners. I've got to go shopping for my mother"; whether mother really did want any shopping done or not was only known to a few very intimate friends of the one who applied for the permission.

The old part of Wendover has really not changed a great deal during the past 50 years. Buildings have had their fronts altered a little here and there but, taken as a whole, everything is much the same as I remember them. I can just remember when there were only about six houses in Perry Street, all at the lower end and Chiltern Road also has been built during my time.

The only actual building that has been added to the old part is The Bank; this site was a garden somewhat higher than the road level with a wall to keep it from encroaching on to the path. There is one other new building, that is the house and shop owned by Mr Syd White in Aylesbury Street. In passing I might mention that it is Aylesbury Street as far as Wharf Road and Aylesbury Road beyond that point.

There are one or two items which may be of interest relating to Wendover which go back far beyond my memory or for that matter, beyond any living memory, which I think I will add to the chapter.

Oh yes! I can hear the inevitable queries, How do you know all this? Well here is the answer. I have always been deeply interested in old places and local history so, when I was much older, in fact it is not more than seven or eight years ago, I used to talk to two men, one was James Abrams, the present Mrs Woolmer's father and the other, Thomas Collings, the present Miss Florence Collings' father. Both were old men and both used to come down my yard on most days during the warmer weather to watch the work going on. They would sit just inside the wood shop, side by side on a trestle and talk, and the conversation would inevitably turn to some person or place known to them in earlier years. Or failing this, if I had time, I would raise a controversial subject, relating to some old buildings in the town on purpose to start them off, and it nearly always got to this: "Now I remember hearing my grandfather say that his grandfather told him" and so on, and, my word, what you could hear about old Wendover and its inhabitants would fill volumes.

Well to return to the items mentioned, first there is a garden just at the bottom of Tring Road now used by Mr Guntrip and next to it is a house called Holly Cottage. Somewhere on the site of this house or just inside the garden, I cannot say for sure, stood a church, known as Saint John's which was, according to Mr Fred Slade, "only a chapel of ease" attached to the adjacent nunnery, or convent. This church has been the subject of many discussions but Mr Slade received something of a shock when levelling the lower part of his garden to make a croquet lawn. This lawn is close to the site of the old church and on digging it for levelling purposes, Mr Slade and his man unearthed human bones, thus proving that it had stood in its own churchyard. The story goes that, so many people attended this church rather than walk all the way to the parish church that the vicar of those times "pulled the strings" and got it demolished.

The convent spoken of above was the building now occupied by Dr McConnell, in that part of Wendover known as "Paradise". This has always been known in my day as Hazeldene House and is a peculiarly built house altogether. Built in the shape of a letter "L" it has a number of small rooms upstairs all leading off one long passage, while the large room now used as a dining room situated in that part of the "L" which runs towards the old water mill was once a large kitchen with flagstone floor, complete with very

Wheelwrights, Watering Cans and Witchell

old oven and a large stone-built copper similar to those in old farmhouses which were used for brewing.

At the spot where the surgery window now looks out towards Tring Road was a door which was approached by two or three steps running up by the wall. I can remember these steps and the bricked up doorway can still be seen. The old people told of many strange happenings in and around this old house, of hauntings, doors opening and what not. My stepmother lived at this house in her young days as sewing maid and she vouched for some of these tales being true. The path lined with old trees which leads into Tring Road was spoken of by old people as "Nuns Walk"; it is said that not only did they use the path as an approach to St John's Church, but were accustomed to stroll up and down there for exercise. There is also the remains of a similar path and row of trees on the other side of the house, and which no doubt was also used by the nuns. Regarding queer happenings in the vicinity of this strange old house, I personally had a very strange experience quite close to there. At first I was afraid to tell anyone for fear of ridicule, but at last, I told my stepmother; she in turn got me to tell her brother, the late Mr Frank Eldridge, and to my great amazement and somewhat to my relief he said that he had met with the same experience many years before, but enough of these strange things for the present.

Another link with even much older times is the place now called Bucksbridge. This spot is said to be where the deer used to come to from the great stretches of woodland on and around the Boddington Hill and Hale Road districts to drink at the stream and was originally known as "Bucks Furlong", the name taken by Miss Wyrlie-Birch for her house.

Hale Farm was the ancient home of the Collet family; Dean Collet, first Dean of St Paul's was of this family. Many of this family's remains lie in Wendover Churchyard.

Another very ancient building is Wellwick House, a farm lying to the west of the town itself, well out in the fields. A fine piece of architecture and well preserved, lovely to look at from the outside, it has an eerie atmosphere inside. For those who are sensitive to such an atmosphere it is worth a visit. This atmosphere cannot be wondered at if all the legends are true. The infamous judge of the Bloody Assizes, Judge Jefferies, once lived there and it is said that this old house is connected by an underground tunnel to Chequers Court. This farm was in the hands of the Billington family for many years. I knew all the younger generation and have heard many tales of the much discussed Wellwick Ghost from them as well as from employees on the farm but, never having met the apparition myself, cannot say much about it.

With regard to the supposed tunnel, when the Billington family left Wellwick it was taken over by a Mr Dell, and the whole farm was purchased by the late Sir John Lawson-Walton, one time Attorney General and who built Coombe House. He caused excavations and soundings to be made and had experts down to see the place but no one ever heard that any discoveries were made. RAF pilots report that at certain times of the year the vegetation in the fields show signs of a line from Wellwick in the direction of Chequers Court similar to vegetation grown on shallow soil but that is as far as one can get towards discovering the tunnel.

This old farm in mentioned in the records of the hedging and ditching and splitting up of the common lands. It is stated as having been then in the possession of Henry Deering Esq., who received 223 acres as his share of the split up of the common possession. It is interesting to note that a certain Thomas Mellison received the wonderful amount of 1 perch, while Lord Hampden received "four acres for his manorial rights – nine acres for his share of the greater tithes, and 400 acres for his demesne lands", altogether 413 acres of land which up to that time was land common to the use of all men for the grazing of their few sheep or pigs.

An allotment of 11 perches was valued at 2s.0½d per year in those days. Compare the price today against the value of money in those days and Lord Hampden and Henry Deering, together with a few others, at once became rich men and all at the expense of the peasant classes. I am not a Communist by any means but all this really makes me wonder.

In the days of the Turnpike Gates, one gate was at the spot where the London Road forks off past Well Head; the old gatekeeper's garden with the remains of the well can still be seen on the left bank of the road when leaving Wendover. There was a workhouse somewhere on the London Road but owing to conflicting reports I cannot say where it stood. One of the old men whom I mentioned earlier in this chapter used to say that it was situated just this side of the site of the toll gate while the other claimed that it was just about where Smalldean railway bridge now is. The only guide is that the road now known as Gravel Pit Hill was known to the old people as Workhouse Hill but, as I've said, whether the workhouse actually stood at the top of the bottom of the hill no one seems to be able to rightly decide.

Chapter 6

Personalities

So far, I have devoted much time to describing buildings and the surrounding district, so for the next few paragraphs I will try to focus the reader's attention on several of the outstanding personalities of the Wendover of my childhood. Naturally, as far as I was concerned, my parents were the most important people on earth and, as I have said next to nothing about my mother, I will start with a word picture of her.

Elizabeth Anne Rayner was born in the year 1861 in an old thatched house which stood in an old fashioned orchard at Terrick, not far from the crossroads and just opposite to the old farm house. A kind of moat ran right round the house which was approached by a rickety old rustic bridge. A large tree stood just outside the back door. The tree still stands there but the moat has long since dried up and vanished.

I have heard my mother say that, as a child, she used to sail round this moat in a flat-bottomed, half-tub, half-boat kind of craft with her brothers and their friends, who were children of a retired army doctor and Crimean War veteran named Lennard. The trouble always came when negotiating the rustic bridge because everybody had to lie flat to pass underneath it and as the boat was never very dry on the bottom their nice clean frocks and pinafores always came off very badly. It was at this house that a terrible misfortune overtook my mother's family.

The oldest son, William, had started work at Garner's bakery, Aylesbury and was about 15 years old. He came home one Saturday complaining of a bad throat: this proved to be diphtheria and within a few days he was dead. Added to this, all the rest of the family as well as a small nephew who was staying with them and who came from London, with the exception of my mother and her youngest brother, had contracted the dread disease and within about eight or nine days, four children as well as the nephew had died. Their little bodies lie in Ellesborough Churchyard, the spot being marked by a small stone cross. There is still one person living who can remember this sad event.

Before leaving this old house I will add that it was used as a butcher's shop by my grandfather and after the terrible happenings spoken of above it was decided to pull it down. The property belonged to the Rothschild family and the house and shop now occupied by Mr Claydon (the shop has been closed down for some years now) was built especially for my grandparents to move into.

My mother was a well-built woman, slightly above the average height of women, with dark brown hair which was always done in a bun at the back, bright blue eyes which twinkled and sparkled when she laughed and dimples in her cheeks which in her younger days added an impishness to her looks.

Her complexion was clear and of the "roses and cream" kind which even in these days would certainly need no make-up. As for personality, she seemed to overflow with fun and had an extreme sense of humour. Altogether my mother was in every sense a very fine and healthy-looking woman, liked by all who had any dealings with her but alas, for all her healthy looks she was in reality never well, as a matter of fact I never remember her being well for many weeks at a time and when she passed away in 1909 the doctors proclaimed her as a woman of 48 with the insides of a woman of 70. I have no doubt whatever that had she lived in these enlightened days of advanced surgery her life would not only have been prolonged but would have been much happier. As it was she had a great sympathetic understanding for anyone who suffered and would go to almost any length to help. This was the mother to whom I own my life and who was everything in the world to me.

I have already spoken of my father's character in the first chapter and will only add here that as long as he lived he was one of the best husbands and father who ever breathed, I cannot say more.

As for people outside my family, the most outstanding personality was the then Lord of the Manor, and vicar of the parish, the Rev. Albert Smith, father of the present Lord of the Manor, General Lionel Abel-Smith, the family having adopted the double name since the Great War. In those days the vicarage was almost the centre of everything. The Misses Helen and Maud Smith assisted in most of the social events of the parish and were loved by all. Compare the vicarage of those days to the present time; the indoor servants numbered six consisting of cook, housemaid, parlourmaid, kitchen maid, second housemaid and butler, while the outdoor staff was coachman, stableboy-footman, two gardeners and an odd man who cleaned boots and assisted generally.

The vicar, a tall man with a ginger-coloured beard and hair which was rapidly turning white, was a very strict but very kind-hearted man: he would give very liberally to anything in the parish and to any poor person. His kind-heartedness was such that he could never see any harm in anyone and this led to his being deceived on many occasions. His coachman could tell many tales of the women in one particular locality who would set their children to watch for the vicar's carriage while they were at the wash tub, but by the time the vicar had arrived the woman would be sitting beside an almost empty grate, wrapped in a shawl with an open Bible lying on the table.

I have received several presents from the Smith family, the foremost in my mind at the moment being a big box of trains, consisting of engine, tender and a whole lot of carriages all painted different colours. Vastly different from the present-day toy trains, the engine was just a piece of green tin bent over and resembled the outlines of the 'Rocket', but I thought worlds of that train and played with it for years, putting a piece of paper in the chimney to represent smoke and pulling the whole thing with a piece of string. To get some idea of the size of this toy, each carriage was roughly 3" by $1\frac{1}{2}$" as was also the engine and tender. What would the child of today think of it?

The Church was beautifully kept and everything very orderly: no vestments or processional cross but the choir boys were provided with so many new Eton collars a year and a bright red bow and each summer a new straw hat with a blue band. The collars and bows had to be worn in church, in fact, as soon as a boy became older and began to wear a 'stand-up' collar he was gently but firmly told that "his voice was going" or some other excuse to tell him to get out.

Each man had a large hymn-book, Ancient and Modern and a nice Psalter. The cassocks were black and it was a recognised thing to have clean surplices at Easter, Harvest Festival and Christmas. The strength of the choir was ten men and sixteen boys, all well trained by their choir master, Mr Bushell, the schoolmaster. Only two of the men choristers of those days are still alive: they are Mr Fred Slade, the present organist and Mr Maurice Franklin, tenor and bass respectively. The bells were "chimed" instead of being "rung" as now, owing to the tower not being strong enough to stand the strain and it was not until 1914 that real ringing was carried out, after the tower had been reinforced and a new bell added.

I have already mentioned Mr John George Bushell the old schoolmaster, but these memoirs would not be at all complete without further reference to that man to whom so many Wendover men and women owe so much. He was a man of medium height, well built and of upright carriage. As I knew him he was grey haired, with a red face and a white moustache and a habit of sniffing, screwing his face round to one side at the same time.

He was a very stern but very just schoolmaster and although he was not a great favourite during schooling days there are very few indeed who speak ill of him now that they are old enough to look back and understand all he has meant to them in after years. It is interesting to note that he came to Wendover and opened a private school at what is now known as Chiltern

House, Aylesbury Street. There he taught boys who are now old men, in fact many of them have passed on. One of these was Mr George Adams who, after my grandfather died, became owner of the Laurels, Little Kimble. He can best be described to the younger generation as Reg Webb's grandfather.

I don't know what year it was when Mr Bushell took over Wendover Church Schools, but he retired at Easter 1907, (the same time that I left school) and he died in 1916.

As I write this many old people come before my mental vision, especially do I see them dressed in their Sunday clothes on their way to and from Church or Chapel. So regular were they in their habits and so precise in the time of arriving at their places of worship that one could almost set a clock by them. This is brought home very clearly when I remember how I used to watch for one old man coming home from church so that my mother would know just when to start taking up the Sunday dinner to be ready for when my father arrived home from Church.

The names of some of these old men won't convey much to the younger generation as they have passed on, leaving no children, but I feel I must write at least three of their names, all Church people. First Mr Harry Malins, a boot repairer; secondly Mr Alfred Perrin, another boot repairer, both very smart in their silk hats and frock coats; and thirdly James Ives, yard man at the Red Lion, spick and span in a black suit, cut in the old fashioned way with a long jacket, and the sleeves, pockets and all edges bound with black braid and a well brushed black felt billycock hat, something like the modern porkpie but with a black band round it fastened with a small bone buckle.

I have so far dealt with people who were very punctual and who more or less corroborated the clocks.

There was however, one old couple who lived at the cottage now occupied by Mr H West in Pound Street, who also in their own way really let you know something of the time on a Sunday morning. They were Mr Joel Bedford and his wife: they used to attend the Congregational chapel and were invariably late, so it came that when one saw them going to Chapel one knew it was past 10.30am.

Chapter 7

Neddy, Soldier, Foxy and Jacob

In the last chapter I spoke of outstanding personalities of Wendover during my childhood, all of whom were well known in their several spheres of life and all classes as respectable townsfolk.

What I am about to say next is not meant to be unkind in any way to anyone but I can't pass without adding a few lines about some old and rather amazing personalities who lived during my early school days. Four old men stand out very clearly in my mind and a queerer set would be very difficult to find, especially in these days. Their names, as I knew them, were Edwin 'Neddy' Collings, 'Soldier' Dancer, 'Foxy' Foskett and Jacob Eggleton. But we'll take them one by one.

Neddy Collings lived at No 1 Back Street with his wife, who was as opposite to Neddy as it was possible to be. She was a short, rather fat, old lady with a very cheery, round red face. She wore very old-fashioned spectacles, a black lace mob cap and her hair, which still retained its dark colour, hung in 'corkscrew' curls down to her shoulders. A black skirt and bodice on which was a handmade lace collar, held together with a large old fashioned brooch, and a small black apron competed her make-up. Neddy was a very tall old man who walked with the aid of a stick owing to one leg being bent sideways somehow. He invariably wore an old frock coat which had long since discarded its blackness for a number of shades of greenish grey. He had a short beard and long hair which tousled out from beneath a battered bowler hat in winter or a straw hat which defied description in summer. His boots were usually held together by odd bits of boot lace and his face had the appearance of not being on speaking terms with soap and water.

A short filthy-looking clay pipe was always in his mouth whether full and alight or absolutely empty and what he used for tobacco to smoke in it was nobody's business. I have heard it said on many occasions that he used to take the tea out of the tea caddy at the Kings Head when the landlady wasn't looking and smoke it. One thing I can actually vouch for is that if ever he heard that a shepherd had set a new sheep fold anywhere near he would visit the scene and cut off lengths of the new tarred cord which was always used to tie the hurdles together, so that he could smoke it in his pipe.

Now comes the queerest part about this old man: his habit was to sit on the stone seat near the drinking fountain at the Town Clock. As I have already said his pipe was always in his mouth and he had the queer habit of always sitting with the forefinger of one hand, I forget which hand, pushed into the bowl of the pipe whether the tobacco was alight or not. He had done this for so long that the end of the finger was blackened and charred almost as far as the bottom of the nail. I have been laughed at for telling this story several times but it is true because I, with other boys, used to get pieces of tarred cord and give it to him if he would show us his finger.

I did not know quite so much about either of the other three old men but the picture of them stands out clearly in my mind. 'Soldier' Dancer lived in the old cottages close to Mr S White's shop, which stand facing the clock tower. He was a short, old man with a thin wrinkled face and he walked very badly, having a badly bent leg. His story to us boys was that he had been a soldier and was wounded but I cannot say if this was true or not. He always wore a brown velvet jacket with brass buttons and cap with 2 peaks (back and front) which rather amused us. I remember that he used to crack jokes to make the other old men laugh.

'Foxy' Foskett was the roughest and dirtiest of them all. He was a heavily built man with a flabby face. The colour of his complexion was bluish purple, mostly concealed by dirt. He was always dressed in a dirty grey suit which hung on him anyhow and made his shoulders look more round than ever. He loped along with his hands stuffed deep into his trousers pockets: altogether he was a fat, dirty and utterly repulsive individual.

The last of this queer quartet was an old man named Jacob Eggleton. He lived in Bacombe Terrace and was great uncle to the present Percy Eggleton. In dress, habits and personality he was so much unlike the others that one wondered why he was always with them. This old chap was always clean and tidy, he walked along rarely speaking to anyone, sometimes he would be smoking, but I never knew him smoke anything but real tobacco.

Jacob was supposed to be very religious and therefore he was always regarded as being 'not quite all there'. I remember that my mother used to give him odd things, such as packets of tea or anything in the edible line and to hear this poor old fellow pour out his thanks, always ending with "The Lord will reward you, mam" was enough to bring tears to one's eyes.

These four old men could always be found on the stone seats by the drinking fountain passing remarks about the people who passed by. These remarks were never very complimentary. Mr Bushell was always telling the children that they were not to stop and talk to these old men. I used to wonder why, but since I have been older I know the answer. My opinion is that Wendover is well rid of men such as the first three.

While these old men were sitting on one seat, another old man used to sit on the other seat. His name was Eggleton, some relation to Jacob, but very

34

different from those four just mentioned. He was a Crimean War veteran, but would not tell us children anything about it, neither would he join in the rough jokes of the other old men. Talking of his being an old war veteran brings another old man, also a veteran soldier, to my mind. His name was Woodley and was Peter Powell's grandfather, a very wiry old man, quick in movement and speech. I believe he was a veteran of the Zulu War and I have heard my father say that when this old man had had a pint or two of beer he would begin pointing in front of him and shouting, "Here they come boys, stand firm, we shall beat 'em," and so on. Of course this was in the days when beer was real beer and not, as Lord Woolton now says, 90 percent water. Also it was 2d per pint for mild and 3d for best bitter, so it did not cost much or take much to make men begin to talk.

While still on the subject of personalities of my childhood days, I would like to mention one named George Blow. He lodged in London Road with the old Mrs Hopcraft, mother of Joe Hopcraft.

A tall man, rather bad on his feet and hard of hearing. He was of a very quiet and inoffensive disposition and did odd jobs for anyone. At that time there was no fishmonger's shop in Wendover and the people had to rely on fishmongers from other towns who came round sometimes with a cart.

George Blow hit on the idea of selling a few bloaters and kippers from a bucket to people whom he knew, but as time went on this increased to other kinds of fish and he had a truck made to push it round in.

I well remember looking forward to my mother buying a kipper for me. He always called at my home but sometimes he would come and in a very quiet voice would say "I thought I'd call Mrs Floyd, but I ain't got none of your kind today, they're a bit salt".

George Blow held the position of lamp lighter for a number of years: that of course was in the days when the street lamps were lit by gas. It was considered a real pastime to watch the lamplighter and boys used to follow a short distance to see three or four lamps lit.

The lamplighter carried a pole about the same size as a broom handle. At one end was a brass tube, the top of which fitted on like the cap of a fountain pen and had holes in the sides, inside this tube was a piece of special tow which was lit and glowed with a smouldering red. A hook fitted on this tube was used to pull the small chain which turned on the gas and then it was ignited by the smouldering tow in the brass tube.

So slow was this method of lighting the street lamps that at certain seasons when the evenings were fairly short, by the time George Blow had finished his lighting up it was almost time to begin extinguishing them again. In later years a younger man had the job and travelled round on a bicycle. The present system of lighting by electricity was introduced in the 1920s.

In these days it seems strange to look back and remember the different kinds of food that used to be peddled from door to door. Three of these were brought by three old men known to me as the Hog Pudding man, the Soft-Cheese man and the Green Tea man. I do not know what the latter commodities were like or the names of the persons who sold them, but I well remember considering it a great treat to have a Hog Pudding for Saturday nights supper made and brought round by a man named Jasper Robins who lived at what is now known as "Homeleigh" near the Police Station. Another old man named Tommy Adams, a little wizened old chap with long hair and a beard, used to come round with either a few herrings or some oranges or both. My father's favourite tale of this old man was how he called one day at the old wheelwrights shop and going up to my father said, "I've called today Mr Floyd, but…" then turning round and seeing Thomas Collins, who was out of work at the time, sitting on the other bench, he whispered, "You don't want any of these bloaters, Mr Floyd, they ain't too good". He went straight over to Collins and said, "Would you like to buy a few very nice bloaters today Tom, nice and fresh". Tom Collins's remarks can best be imagined for he had overheard the whisper.

Wendover had two postal deliveries in those days, 6.30am and 10.30am, the mail being brought by horse and cart (a very high box type of cart, painted red with the usual Royal Cypher) from Tring.

Regularly at just about 6am this cart could be heard pulling up at Freeman's and then the big doors spoken of earlier would open and with much discussion as to the weather prospects, the mail bags for Wendover were unloaded by the postmen and the mail cart would be driven off over the hills to Risborough, to return in the evening to pick up the outgoing mails.

Chapter 8

Church Farm

Church Farm, Little Kimble, stands, as I have already stated, close to the pretty little church at the foot of Great Kimble hill and was part of the Chequers Court estate. At the same time I talk of now my grandfather rented it from the Astley family who were the owners of Chequers. This family, to give it its full name, Frankland-Russell-Astley, was a very old one and claimed a connection with Oliver Cromwell who, it is said, once lived at Chequers. This statement is often denied by those who claim to know history. True, no mention can ever be found of that fact in our school history books but it is certain that the ancient mansion contains a number of Cromwell's relics and there is also a small stained glass window or brass plate, I forget which, behind the organ of Ellesborough Church to the memory of a daughter of Oliver Cromwell or her offspring.

In much later years when I became a Scout Master I became very friendly with the Earl of Buckinghamshire who is a kinsman of the great John Hampden, who in his turn was a cousin of Cromwell. The Earl says that it is perfectly true that Chequers was once the home of Cromwell and also claims that his home, Hampden House, was at one time connected to Chequers by an underground tunnel.

I am only mentioning this as a point of interest, but to revert back to the Astley family I can just remember old Lady Astley, a tall stately old lady with white hair and an aristocratic face. Her eldest son, Mr Bertrand Astley, was a real gentleman and ran the estate for his mother until his death at a fairly early age. The last of the family was Delaville Astley, a young man who threw in his lot with the pioneers of aviation and lost his life at a flying exhibition at Belfast in 1913. He had given his exhibition of flying and was landing when something went wrong; he could have landed safely but would probably have killed many people so he decided to crash on the far side of the crowd. So ended the last male member of a very old and stately family, whose vault can be seen near the west end of Ellesborough Church.

Another member of the Astley family was a clergyman and held the living of Ellesborough but owing to his rather advanced ideas, which were called very high church but which in these days would be considered very moderate, he was not very popular. He had married a widow named Lady Sutton whose son, Sir Richard Sutton, then only a boy, was reputed to be one of the richest land owner of that time, owning almost the whole of Piccadilly besides country estates.

I well remember seeing him riding around the Chequers park and the meadows of Church Farm on his pony accompanied by a groom mounted on a fine hunter. During the winter months this boy always wore a black respirator over his mouth when riding, much to the amazement and amusement of the boys of the surrounding villages. I remember being very jealous of Sir Richard Sutton and would hide myself away for what I used to call "a think" when I would daydream that I was galloping over the meadows on a wonderful pony accompanied by a most wonderful groom.

Church Farm house is an old building which has had a new wing attached: the front faces towards the meadows. As you entered the back door you found yourself in the back kitchen, a longish narrow room with tiled floor, a wide 'dog iron' fire¡place, a large copper, a long sink and a pump all on the left hand or outside wall with a window over the sink which looked out into a large garden with bee hives standing quite close.

At the end of the kitchen was a door which led down two steps into the dairy, which was below ground level and about which I shall have more to say later on.

From this dairy another door led down to the cellar. I have never forgotten the cold claminess of that cellar or of the earthy smell of it. I was always too afraid to go down there without someone to go with me. This, by the way, was where the well-known home-made wine and cider was always stored. Just opposite the sink in the back kitchen was a door which opened into what was called the living kitchen, actually the back kitchen was always known in the old Bucks fashion as the "back house".

Let me give you a picture of that living kitchen. Imagine yourself just entering a fair-sized well-lighted room. As you stand on the threshold, the left hand wall is about two feet away from you, at the other end of this wall is a door leading into the front hall. In the wall facing you is a large, long window looking out over the front flower garden into the meadows. On the right is a large fireplace with big oven and boiler and a high mantlepiece. This fireplace is flanked on either side with a narrow window, the lower half of which is whitened with paint to represent a curtain. The wall along your right hand is plain.

The furnishing is simple. Immediately on your left in the corner stands a Windsor chair, then a big mangle followed by another chair. Many times have I sat on the handle of the mangle and had a swing, much to the consternation of my grandmother lest I should smash my fingers in the cog wheels. One or two chairs stand under the long window on the far side and on the wall between this window and the wall in which is the fireplace, is hung an old fashioned gun rack on which is slung a gun, a rifle and a small cartridge satchel. Under this gun rack stands my grandfather's high backed arm chair and, as the fireplace is built slightly into the room, a narrow cupboard is built on either side under the two small windows. On one of these is a pile of account books, a box or two of cartridges, a cigar box and various objects one would expect to find in a farmhouse.

The mantle shelf is adorned by some old-fashioned brass candlesticks, a very old spice box which unscrews into four parts and a couple of small china ornaments. The other cupboard carries a work basket, a very old fashioned tea caddy, a work box and other signs of a woman's presence, while in the middle stands a big double burner oil lamp, the only means of illumination. A large wicker easy chair completes that corner.

The wall on your right is almost bare but for a bureau, carefully locked but highly polished. The only signs of floor covering is a large, home made rag rug in front of the fire which has a high fender complete with highly polished steel top and fire-irons. The remainder of the floor is plain boards scrubbed daily and then carefully sprinkled with bright silver sand which was always sifted over the floor. A good, solid kitchen table set in the centre of the floor completes the picture with perhaps the addition of some brightly coloured curtains.

On passing from the living kitchen you come into the front hall with the front door, a large cupboard and a window on the right of the stairs and the large pantry door on the left, with the stuffed stag's head on the wall and the dining room directly in front of you. To reach the new wing you had to go through the dining room into a small hall from which a door led out to towards the little church, Another door led into a room which was very rarely used, and another flight of stairs led up to two bedrooms and through a half glass door (frosted glass) onto the main landing. These other bedrooms opened on this landing and another flight of stairs led to the attic. All this description may seem to be unnecessary and to lead to nowhere, but I mention it all now so that later anecdotes will be clearer to understand.

For instance, the attic was a wonderful place to me. As I have stated, my grandparents kept a shop while at the *Bear and Cross* and there were large boxes of small fancy goods which had been brought away when they left and it was a tremendous treat for me to be taken up there and allowed to rummage about in these boxes.

As time went on I was allowed to go up to the attic by myself but one day I was on my way up when I looked along the landing and was surprised to see someone looking at me through the frosted glass door. I remember looking hard at the face which appeared to be pressed close to the glass, as I didn't know who it was I went downstairs and told my mother and grandmother about it. I remember seeing them look queerly at each other and being told something about it being Alice the maid who I had seen there. I knew this to be wrong as Alice was still in the back kitchen, but anyhow the landing and the attic was strictly out-of-bounds to me after that.

It was not until years afterwards that I learned the strange story of a previous tenant of Church Farm. It appears that the house was occupied by an old woman, a recluse who had been disappointed in love or something and who had shut herself away from the world for the rest of her life, vowing that she would not see anyone except a woman who ran the house and looked after her. It appears that there were strange stories about the happenings in the vicinity of those back rooms after this old woman's death. I never really got hold of the truth as to what was really supposed to happen but some of these strange things were told to my grandparents by an old Sister of Mercy known as Sister Gertrude who I knew very well and who used to rent two of those back rooms from my grandmother. I came to the conclusion long ago that the face I saw was something connected to those strange happenings.

I cannot finish the description of Church Farm without mentioning two things, first the door knobs. This may sound a bit strange but these door knobs stand out so clearly in my memory. They were all larger than average and were made of either earthenware or some kind of composition that represented red marble and I used to love to look at the pretty markings in them.

The second has to do with the former tenant, the old recluse mentioned earlier, and is an anecdote that my grandfather loved to relate. The old lady was a Miss Field commonly known as Nannie Field and as I have said before she had shut herself from the world, vowing never to be seen by anyone except her faithful maid.

You will recall that my grandfather was a butcher in his earlier years and also that he was something of a daredevil: anything in the way of harmless mischief was his delight. One day while talking with some friends, the case of Nannie Field was brought up and he boasted that if he wanted to, he could see the old lady face to face. Wagers were laid then and there and so it came about that the next time he called for orders he very unceremoniously pushed passed the astonished and somewhat aged maid and reached the foot of the stairs. Imitating the maid's voice he called to Miss Field that "the butcher was there and what was she to order". So well did he imitate the maid that sure enough the old recluse came to the head of the stairs to give her orders. It only remains to say that my grandfather won his wager and the reputation of being the one outside person to see Nannie Field.

Chapter 9

Animals at Church Farm

I may be rather biased in my views but still I maintain that Church Farm, Little Kimble, is one of the most beautiful spots in the County. Take a look at it from any angle, from the meadow in front of the house if possible, and you'll agree that the house, the Church and the farm buildings together with the great elm trees make a wonderful picture.

Speaking of trees, in my young days there were many more elm trees around that spot, some of which were very large with hollow trunks which made fine homes for the owls which lived there in large numbers and of which I always had a wholesome fear.

The farm building were built to form a square with what was called the Farm Yard in the middle and the ground between these and the road was called the Rick Yard.

These buildings consisted of a large barn with a bin or sunken portion where either corn could be stored or cattle could be kept in the warm and a harness room partitioned at the other end. A second large barn bounded the west end of the Farm Yard. This barn had a threshing floor where corn, but chiefly peas and beans in my day, was threshed by means of an old fashioned flail. It was then put through a winnowing machine to blow the chaff away from the grain. I well remember an old man named Will Rutland threshing in that barn. It was dangerous to stand and watch as the beans would often fly in different directions with great speed and they hurt if one hit you on the face. This old man invited me to try my hand with the flail once, with the result that I hit myself a resounding whack on the back of my head, much to the delight of the old thresher. I've never tried my hand with the flail since.

On the south side of the farm yard stood the stables and the cowhouse and a granary and open shed completed the square.

A large field gate, painted white and hung on a very large gate post, led from the Rick Yard into the Farm Yard and beside this was a long drinking trough fed by an old fashioned pump. The whole farm was infested with rats and in the summer evenings just after dusk my grandfather would stick either a lighted candle or an old fashioned lantern on the top of this large gate post, and lay a trail of chicken food from the foot of the post towards the back door of the house. He would then get hidden behind the low fence which surrounded the house and wait until a large number of rats came out to feed on the food he had put down. Then he would let fly with both barrels of his gun straight along the line of rats. I have seen as many as fifteen to twenty rats killed at one go in this way.

Talking of rats reminds me of one which used to be treated almost as a pet. The cowhouse was built in the usual old-fashioned way with unprepared timber; branches of trees just sawn down the middle formed the framework of the building with boards nailed to the outside. These rough pieces of timber made great rat-runs and the one in question would come out and sit on a beam as soon as milking began. He was a large rat and almost completely white; whether this was due to age or whether he was an Albino I don't know, but the man who did the milking, a certain Bert Badhams, would get a saucer of milk and stand it on the floor, and as soon as rat saw it, down the rough timber he would come and drink it while the cows were being milked, very much to my grandfather's dislike, although he never offered to kill this particular rat.

It was in this very cowhouse that I made my first attempt at milking, an occasion which I shall never forget. My grandfather bought a dear old Jersey cow called Chilton. She was as tame as a kitten and as I used to fondle her and ride on her back I was allowed to call her my cow.

The day came when my request to be allowed to milk her was granted. I was only about six years old so couldn't do much damage. Great preparations were made: a low milking stool and a small polished milk pail and everything was ready. How proudly I marched into the cowhouse and under the watchful eye of Bert was told to begin. This I did only to be greeted by roars of jeering laughter and many rude remarks for I had sat down on the wrong side of the cow. There isn't much wrong in this but it tickled Badhams and the other farm hands to death and I ran from the cowhouse crying bitterly. It was a long time before I tried to milk a cow again but I have never forgotten which is the right side of a cow to sit at for milking and it was even a longer time before Badhams let me forget the incident, which to his simple mind was a huge joke. Now reader, which is the correct side of a cow to milk from? I'll bet you don't know?

Other animals with which I was very friendly were a small donkey and a very big St Bernard dog. I forget their names but I know I used to ride on both of them. I must tell of the incident which was laughed about for many a day in the Kimble household.

A frequent visitor to Church Farm, especially during the summer, was a certain Mr Summers, a fish buyer for the then great London firm of William Whiteley. He would often spend a holiday with his wife and son, Alfie Summers, at the farm, sometimes driving down from London in a very smart dog cart drawn by a tandem of two high stepping horses. A tandem, by the way, is one horse in front of the other.

42

Wheelwrights, Watering Cans and Witchell

Mr Summers was not very tall but was rather stout with a round, red jolly face and a 'corporation' which, when dressed properly was encased in a spotless white waistcoat. He was very fond of walking across the meadows and through the part known as 'The Boxes', owing to the number of Box trees that grow there.

It so happened that one hot summer Sunday afternoon he decided to talk the walk. Of course I wanted to go with them but as it was considered too far for me to walk it was suggested that we should take the donkey and Alfie and I were to take turns in having a ride.

Off we went across what is known as the 'Great Gardens' till the wooded parts were reached. Here the path became steep and very narrow and my parents, Mrs Summers, Alfie and the rest moved into this narrow path, single file. I was riding the donkey at the time and so brought up the rear with Mr Summers walking immediately in front leading the donkey with a short halter.

Now this donkey had a habit of biting anyone he didn't like, and he did this by pinching little bits with his front teeth and whether he disliked the man who held the halter or whether the well-filled trousers seat looked tempting I don't know but he just took a nip at that seat with agonising results for Mr Summers.

That was not all, the donkey took another nip and another, and another; what a to do! The rest of the party in front stopped Mr Summers from getting away, the path was too narrow to step sideways and if he had struck the donkey I should have fallen off. The consequence was, he had to walk backwards up the steep path, constantly keeping the donkey from biting again and narrowly missing tripping backwards over the tree roots. His condition on reaching open ground can best be imagined.

His son, Alfie, was a few years older than me and he died at the age of about 20 following an ear operation.

In the Rick Yard and close to the large barn doors was what was known as a Horse Gear. This is a large iron frame work about three feet high, fixed into the ground in the centre of which is a big flat wheel with cogs on the underside. A spindle from this wheel comes up through the top of the framework and fixes on to an iron socket into which a pole, about twelve to fourteen feet long, tapering from about six inches square to roughly three inches round, is fixed.

A horse is then harnessed to this pole and is driven slowly round and round. As he goes round the cogs on the flat wheel engage a small cog-wheel which is keyed on to a shafting that runs just above ground level into the barn where another shafting takes up the revolutions and so works a chaff cutter, mangold wurzel pulper or any other farm machinery. I have had many rides on the pole of this machine both when the horse was working it and when someone has been pushing it. I used to call it my roundabout. Somewhere in the old boxes which either I or my brother Jack now have is a photograph of Alfie Summers giving me a ride on this old primitive bit of farm machinery. This may not sound a very thrilling game to the present day child but it was a great treat in my young days and stands out clearly in my mind.

Another incident that happened in those days that I shall never forget is when Alfie built a small model of an African mud hut. It was built of twigs and mud with a small doorway and was close to the big barn wall and about six inches high.

It so happened that just as we had got this little hut finished some of the farm hands came to move some straw nearby and, as they did so, out bolted a large rat and made straight for our little mud hut, dodging straight into it, leaving only a bit of his tail outside. Of course the farm hands came along and would have smashed our little hut on purpose to kill the rat, but we begged so hard that we saved it, but I was told that they would give me a penny if I would take hold of the tail and pull the rat out.

I shall never forget the result. I tugged at the rat and out he came but by some means or other slipped the skin off the end of his tail leaving it in my hand while he scampered away. I recall how sick I felt and I did not get my penny.

Chapter 10
Sticky Knickers and Norfolk Suits

I make no apologies for making a lot of Church Farm, for the simple reason that, I always believe, had it not been for the dear old farm, its occupants and the surroundings I should not be here to write all this. As I have said before, I was always ailing as a child but sure enough, although only about three miles away as the crow flies, there was always something in the Kimble air plus the beautiful new milk that always pulled me on to my feet again after an illness.

I thought worlds of my grandparents and would go to almost any length to get a holiday with them and, as my mother was so often ill, I was often sent to stay with them for a few weeks at a time, so it was that quite a lot of my early childhood was spent at Kimble. Who can wonder at my love for that pretty little village.

My grandfather was always a great amateur beekeeper and Church Farm had three hives; the old fashioned straw made type (the present day wooden type of hive was just coming into use).

Not far away, at Askett, between Great Kimble and Monks Risborough, there lived an old man named Messenger, a bootmaker by trade and an expert on bees. He would go for miles to take a swarm of bees or to take the honey from anyone's hives. He could handle bees with as much confidence as ordinary people hold butterflies and I never remember hearing of him being stung.

I watched him on several occasions take the honey from my grandfather's hives, although of course I had to be made up for the occasion with a net mask, gloves, etc., and the mention of honey brings another story to my mind.

The old-fashioned way of extracting honey from the comb was to put the whole comb into a large muslin bag, suspend the bag from a hook in the ceiling or a stick lodged on two high shelves, over a wide earthenware pan. Then give the bag a gentle squeeze to start the honey running and it would gently strain itself through the muslin into the pan. For this my grandfather used an earthenware pan about six inches deep and two feet in diameter used for setting milk in prior to skimming off the cream.

(Now turn back to Chapter Eight to get a picture of the kitchen, especially the corner where my grandfathers chair stood.)

A strong stick is lodging on the cupboard under the little window with its

45

other end on the lowest part of the gun rack. On this stick hangs a large muslin bag from which the golden honey is slowly pouring into the big flat pan.

It is evening and the room is lit by an oil lamp on the table. Gran is sewing by the fire and Gramp is busy with his milk books while the maid, Drucilla Green, known as "Alice" also sits sewing on the other side of the table. Having nothing better to do, I am playing soldiers by myself and marching round the kitchen wearing a little pair of brown check knickers that my mother had made from one of Gramp's old shooting jackets (how well I remember those knickers!)

Of course, childlike there was not room for me to play properly without going behind my grandfather's chair, and under the stick bearing the honey bag. I was scolded and warned but begged for one more march round.

Round I went until I got to the honey, then it happened. Passing under the stick I slipped and sat flop in the pan of honey. Oh the consternation, the scolding and the tears over what I thought to be a ruined pair of nice knickers, I shall never forget it. Neither shall I forget being put to bed, the only time so far as I can remember ever being put to bed for punishment.

One of my great pleasures about these times was playing at being a butcher. My grandfather still had a lot of his butcher's tools such as hooks, stretchers (pieces of wood made to stretch the carcasses of meat open), pulleys and many odds and ends. So I would play, dressed up in a blue apron with a steel hung at my side and an old specially blunted knife. In this way I have stuck and skinned many an old stool or a box, and pole-axed a good number of old chairs. Another game was filling old cartridge cases with sand and using the old-fashioned cartridge filling machines, which I still have. Such games as these will sound queer to the children of today but as I had no-one to play with I always had to make to my own games.

The South African war broke out during the last year that my grandparents lived at Church Farm and I well remember walking to Little Kimble Station each morning to fetch the paper which used to come from Aylesbury about nine o'clock. Fridays were somewhat of a special occasion, for on that day the only picture paper came out. It was known as the *Penny Illustrated Paper* and was full of wonderful pictures of the war, chiefly artists' ideas of what the war was like with bullets making the dust fly up perilously close to the soldiers and here and there a man making a very theatrical kind of collapse when struck by a bullet.

One outcome of this war was an advertisement. I believe it was for some kind of tobacco but am not sure. This advert showed an officer complete with sun helmet, monocle and flowing moustache, standing with his legs

Wheelwrights, Watering Cans and Witchell

wide apart with field glasses in one hand and a shell bursting between his feet while he apparently takes no notice and the inscription was something about being "Cool like the Colonel".

Even in those days one couldn't play about with shells like that but we boys used to gaze at that picture with great ideas of what heroes our soldiers must be. I believe this advertisement can still be seen in the old copies of the book which was printed periodically called *With the Flag to Pretoria*.

This period started my immense liking for toy soldiers, I had already had some to play with but now I wanted more, and as was usual I got them. I would then draw a battlefield in soft chalk on the big dining table and set my soldiers out in battle array. The first soldiers I remember owning were some small ones, they were in a box and the two officers were on horseback, one on a black horse and one on a white horse. I believe the last named is still in existence as is also one of the next box I had that contained a Scottish pipe band.

About this time my mother and grandmother both had to attend a London hospital regularly and so I often had a present, the box of bagpipes was one, the large box of building bricks which is still knocking about was another present. It was at Church Farm that I had my Monkey given to me before I was a year old. I played with this monkey as long as I played with anything and he finished up in pieces long after when my own oldest boy used to have him as a bed companion. When I was young, if a punishment was due it would hurt me more if monkey was smacked, or as my grandfather used to do, sling him against the wall; truly a good friend and a great toy.

One of the great treats of those early days was to be taken up the hill to the little general shop at the *Bear & Cross*. Armed with a penny, which in those days seemed such a big amount, I would gaze longingly at the very few small things that were suitable to play with. I remember two of these purchases very vividly, one was a sheet of scraps or cut out pictures for pasting into a scrap album. Mine was a sheet of pictures of Father Christmas and some of these can still be seen in my old scrapbook. The other was a sheet of transfers of soldiers and South African war scenes. I also remember another occasion when, as there was nothing in the way of toys in the shop, rather than come away without anything, I insisted on buying a small ball of string that was coloured red and white and I well remember the disappointment on reaching home to find that there was nothing I could do with it. Queer how such trivial events stick in ones mind all through life. I expect my own children have often thought me rather unkind when I have tried to stop them from buying things that would cause them disappointment as that string did to me, but that is just the way of a passing comment.

As a diversion it may give the reader something to laugh at, if it was of no other interest, if I here stop and tell something of how children dressed in those days. The boys wore heavy boots, shoes for boys were unheard of, stockings with double thickness knees. These were always worn over the knees and kept there by garters. Trousers were almost always worn about level with the centre of the kneecap or in some cases below the knee when new to allow for growing. These trousers were finished off with two buttons at the bottom, just as the present day sleeves of the jacket. If the cloth was corduroy then the buttons were a kind of rough unpolished brass, as were the jacket buttons. The jackets were much the same as the present but with very narrow collar and reveres. An 'Eton' collar was always worn, usually made of celluloid, and a bow which fastened to the stud with a loop of elastic. It was unheard of to go without a hat so each boy wore a cap with a small peak.

The alternative to this kind of clothes was a Norfolk suit. This consisted of a suit made of a rough tweed. Instead of trousers were knickerbockers (much like the plus-fours of today but not so baggy) and these were always either buttoned below the knee or kept there by elastic. The jacket was buttoned right up to the throat and had a belt round the waist. Owing to my parents' fear for my health, I always had to wear this kind of suit, summer and winter and how I hated it. I well remember how I used to vow that when I grew up I would never wear either a Norfolk Suit or clothes made with a rough cloth. One suit that I had during those early days has always remained in my memory. It was made by my dear mother out of some gingery coloured rough flannel kind of material. It consisted of knickerbockers with elastic round below the knee and a blouse with buttoned cuffs and elastic round the waist. I had to wear this during a hot summer, together with thick double kneed stockings and boots; and as if this was not bad enough, I was crowned with a, wait for it!! yes, a Black Trilby, and all this at the age of six. Do you wonder at me disliking rough cloth for my clothes?

The girls of those days were dressed in frocks closely resembling the present day. Gym slip with sleeves attached, a clean pinafore through the top of which the girls' arms were put and then it was buttoned at the back. Some of these pinafores had "flounces" on the shoulders which were starched and ironed to stand almost upright. The greatest harm one could do to a girl was to either press these flounces down or otherwise make the pinafore dirty, this would always bring down the wrath of the girl's mother very heavily. The hair was always worn long with a band of coloured hair ribbon tied in it one way or another. "Bobbed" hair was unknown but one or two girls had a "Shingle" this was supposed to make the hair grown thicker and stronger. Tam O'Shanters were the usual head wear and the make-up was completed by buttoned boots which often came half way up to the knee.

Chapter 11

Seasons at Church Farm

I hope, reader, you will not tire of my continual mention of Church Farm, but as I have said before, so much of my early life was connected with it that it is hard to cease writing of its memories.

Winter and Summer each had its own highlights, so, for that matter did spring and autumn as far as the farming activities were concerned. For instance, the lambing season was a tremendously joyful time for me, for there was almost always at least one lamb which was either a weakling or whose mother had died and who consequently would be brought indoors to get warm and be fed by a bottle like a baby. I used to love these little lambs and would cuddle them until their struggles forced me to let them go.

I well remember crying bitterly when on one occasion I was allowed to see the lambs tails being cut off. To do this, the poor little beasts were taken to a doorway in the farm buildings that led to the granary and was approached by a stone step. Each lamb was held up by a man and its tail was held across the threshold, which was about two feet above ground level. My grandfather then singled out the correct point in the tail and placed a very sharp knife on the exact spot then, with a small box-wood mallet he would strike the back of the knife and, Bang! Tail gone. I think I cried far louder than all the lambs put together, so much so that I had to be taken indoors out of the way. I have never watched this operation since.

There are of course other Spring and Autumn events but for the purpose of writing I will just class them into the Summer and Winter groups.

Summer – what memories fly through my mind, the long days out in the hay meadows or harvest fields. Sheep shearing in the big meadow known as The Great Gardens, and not at all least, the drops of beer with the men at work in the fields. As long as I can remember I have always been allowed to have a drop of beer. My grandfather's old saying was "water the plants if you want to raise a good cabbage" and he certainly never withheld my drop of "water", so it came about that when in the hay field I always had my drop when the men had theirs.

The beer would be taken out to them in big old fashioned stone bottles or gallon jars as they were called and a number of half-pint mugs made of shiny tin would be slung on a strap or piece of cord. One of these tin mugs, with a particular marking, was mine. Of course I did not have a full half-pint but just a little drop and I have never had anything so nice in my life, and I think it must be due to the experiences that to this very day my favourite drink is beer from a metal drinking vessel and I hope to own a metal drinking mug for my own use one of these days.

There is a story connected with his harvest beer and I may as well tell it now.

In Chapter 8 I mentioned the dairy at Church Farm and promised I would say more about it later on. Well you may remember that I said that this dairy was below ground level to keep it cool and was approached by two steps. Along the right-hand wall was the rack-like table on which the large milk pans stood where the milk was placed to prepare for skimming. At the end nearest the steps the rack was built higher and on this part stood the beer barrels. It so happened that one day one of the barrels gave out and was declared empty. The other barrel was tapped and as I watched this being done I said to my grandfather "May I call the empty one mine, Grampy?" He assented and went away forgetting the incident, but propped the so-called empty cask up at the back ready for a final drain off. I found my little tin mug and began to help myself. I repeated this again and again until finally I curled up in the kitchen and went to sleep. My grandmother, thinking I was ill woke me up only to discover that I could not stand or talk properly, and it was not until a great deal of questioning that she discovered what I had been doing during the afternoon and I had to be carried to bed. It appears that my only explanation was "Well Gran, it doesn't matter if I am a little drunk". This saying was always one of my grandparents chief ways of teasing me right up to the time of their death. Needless to say the dairy was always out of bounds to me after that.

It was during hay-making one year that I had a very narrow escape. There was an old man by the name of Tom Clay, who used to spend the winter in the workhouse and then come out and work during the summer, living and sleeping rough. This old man always came to get a job at Church Farm, and, being a very dirty, tobacco-chewing person with a terrible flow of language when upset, he was the butt of all small boys.

One day, he and a boy named Clarke were working in the meadow known as The Moors, raking the hay into heaps ready to be picked up and I was playing with a ball near to them. Tom Clay was using a heavy draught rake, which is an implement with a rake head about five feet long and large teeth (not used much in these days).

It so happened that my ball fell close to Clarke and as Clay had his back turned, Clarke picked up the ball and flung it at him hitting him behind the head. Clay took one look, and, thinking it was me who had thrown the ball roared that he would kill me and started to run. He was still carrying his big rake but as I turned to run away he flung it at me. The teeth missed my head and body by inches but hooked in the back of my boot bringing me down without injury. I don't know what else would have happened if my grandfather had not heard Clay shouting. He, as usual, had his gun with him and came rushing up vowing he would shoot Tom Clay if he moved another inch towards me.

Both Clay and Clarke were paid off on the spot but I well remember Clay swearing he would set fire to the farm during the night and my grandfather patrolling around with his gun well into the night in case Clay kept his threat. But most of all I remember the severe telling off I got about it all, a telling off which I considered most unjust but I didn't play ball in the hay field again.

It was always considered a great honour to be allowed to ride home on the top of the final load of hay or corn from any particular field or meadow, but to ride home on the very last load of all was really something and that particular load was the object of a great welcome at the farm and always called for an extra drink for the men.

Threshing time was also a great time for me; this was done just the same as it is today and called for great activities in the Rick Yard. Mr James Stevens, grandfather of Mr Sidney Stevens, was the proprietor of a number of these threshing outfits and it was a great thing for me to go out and watch the steam traction engine at work. One thing stands out clearly in my mind. On one occasion the engine driver, a John Green from Weston Turvill, showed me how he cooked his mid-day meal by thoroughly cleaning his long handled fire shovel and frying a rabbit's leg in it in the engine fire box. I thought this was very wonderful especially as one of my favourite dinners in those days was a fried rabbit's leg.

Summer days always bring back memories of the beautiful meadows with the stream and flowering trees in front of the old house and of the pretty picture one could get from these meadows of the farm with the dear little church standing close by. Even in those days I used to try to sketch this picture, but I'm afraid the results of my efforts were always disappointing.

Summer was also the time when young animals were usually born and these were special favourites of mine, and I could never understand why I was not allowed to go and stroke them. I learned one day though, when I was allowed to try to feed a tiny calf with a milky mixture out of a small bucket. All went well until the milk had nearly gone, then the calf began to bunt the bucket to try to get more and in consequence over I went, bucket, calf and all. I was nearly frightened to death to say nothing of the mess I got into.

My grandfather was a great wine and cider maker and of course this again was a summer job at which I always "helped". The cider would be bottled and the corks securely tied down and it was a great delight to my grandfather whenever one of these bottles were opened, to cut the string or wire and let the cork fly out. I remember I would run away and scream if I saw him doing this as the pop made by the cork scared me stiff, much to Gramp's disgust.

Autumn would bring with it one of the outstanding events of the year, the Harvest Home Supper. Several days before this happened there would be great preparations, cooking home cured hams and the roasting of huge joints of beef, pastry-making and similar activities.

When the great evening arrived the big dining table would be brought into the kitchen and loaded with the good things, decorations hung around the room and the two big double-burner oil lamps lit. Then the farm hands and one or two guests would arrive and take their seats. Grandfather would then say grace and with a flourish would commence to carve the cold beef while my father would do the same with the hams; at the same time the women folk would be filling up the glasses or serving the vegetables.

As soon as the feed was over, short speeches were made and toasts drank and then a sing-song usually started off by my father with his old favourite "The Anchor's Weighed". This old song by the way was sung on the wireless not so long ago, the announcer saying that someone had discovered it in Devonshire and that no one else knew it. I was always allowed to stay up to the finish of these suppers so to me it was a really outstanding event.

As Winter came on my outdoor activities got fewer and fewer until the usual Sunday morning visit to Church was almost the only move outside the house, but these days carried before them one big thought, Christmas. Shall I ever forget those Church Farm Christmases?

If at Christmastime I was living at Kimble, the preparations took my attention, but if I should be at Wendover the excitement at the thought of going to Kimble was just terrific. Being the only child my stocking was always well packed but there was something else to add.

My grandfather, as was the custom of the old men of those days, always wore long stockings; they were made of a pale blue stockinette material with a white top and white at the toe and heel and whether I spent Christmas eve at Kimble, or as on one occasion when I had been ill, made the journey on Christmas morning in a horse and closed carriage there was always one of these big stockings crammed full besides my own little stocking. My earliest recollection of this being a large brightly coloured ball sticking out of the top. Toys in those days were vastly different from today with the exception of the table games such as Ludo and Snakes and Ladders. One of the chief toys was a Noah's Ark in which were a number of little wooden animals, but

Wheelwrights, Watering Cans and Witchell

I shall never forget having my first Magic Lantern, phew! how it smoked and what a smell the newly painted tin made as it got hot. Some of the slides belonging to this little lantern are still in existence.

Before I finish the story of Church Farm winters, I must recall something that would truly shock many people. In the cold weather my grandfather always had what he called his "night-cap" before going to bed. This night cap was a real stiff peg of whiskey in a tumbler filled up with hot water, a spoonful of Demerara sugar and a thick slice of lemon. Of course I always had my night cap too in a little glass which I believe I still have. My mouth waters at the thought of these night caps even as I write this.

Whiskey in those days was real whiskey and the price was 3/6d per bottle. My grandfather used to buy it by the gallon in a great stone jar and the price would work out at about 2/6 or 2/8 per pint.

I think I must now leave Kimble for a bit and return to Wendover days, returning to Kimble and "The Laurels" later on in this book.

Chapter 12

Fairs and Shows

This chapter more or less follows on where Chapter 7 left off, but I must first go back to the year 1897 known as Jubilee year. This was the Diamond Jubilee of Queen Victoria. Being then only five years old I cannot remember a great deal of the general festivities but the local ones stand out quite clearly. Firstly, I well remember my father erecting a flag-pole by the front of the old shop and my mother making a large red white and blue flag (like the French flag) out of some bunting material that she bought at Kings draper's shop. Then on the great day a public tea was held in Thompson's orchard and sports held in Marshallway's meadow, mentioned earlier on in connection with the opening of the railway.

All the school children met at the schools and marched to the meadow, headed by the Wendover Band, although I was not yet at school I went with the others. Every child carried a flag and as it was not possible to purchase a Union Jack my father bought an American "Stars and Stripes" for me and made a "posh" stick to attach it to. I still have that American flag.

The tea was a huge success. I remember that my father assisted in the serving and his outsized teapot really took my fancy. Each child had to take its own mug or cup, mine was a mug with a small nursery rhyme and a picture on it. I kept this mug for years as a souvenir but when my father married a second time it, with a good many more of my treasured childhood possessions "went west".

Following the tea, a programme of sports was run. I was too young to compete, but I remember running to the railway fence with a number of other children to watch some platelayers push a railway truck along one of the lines on the siding. Little did we know that they were gong to "fire a salute" with fog signals and I have never forgotten the awful fright I had when the first one went off.

It is strange what funny ideas come into a child's head when young and how memories of those ideas often remain through life. I shall always remember on one of my early Christmas Eves suddenly hearing the hymn "Oh come all ye faithful" being sung out in the street by a choir. On being told that it was the "Waites" and not knowing what that really meant, I at once concluded that the Angelic Host of Bethlehem that my mother had been telling me of had suddenly visited Wendover. That idea and the tune of the grand old hymn has never really left me.

Two dates in each year were eagerly look forward to by children of all ages, these were May 13 and October 2nd. These were the days on which Wendover Fair was held.

May Fair as it was generally called (and still is for that matter) was the annual Cattle Fair, while the October one was only a pleasure fair. On May Fair day, farmers and dealers would arrive with their cattle or sheep soon after nine o'clock and buying, selling or "chopping" would go on until sometime around mid-day, or until everyone had sold or bought what he required.

I have seen Pound Street full of pens of sheep right from London Road to the *Shoulder of Mutton* and London Road packed with cattle. The public houses, open all day in those days, did a roaring trade with the drovers and cattle men, to say nothing of people who used to visit the fair with things to sell. One of these people was a man from Aylesbury who invariably came with two large baskets packed with bunches of radishes. This man had some sort of disease that caused him to have a very large neck and when, as children we heard people say that he had sold his body for medical research when he died, we used to look at him almost spellbound with awe.

Our house was kept as "open house" on May Fair day and quite a number of people, mostly customers of my father, would come in for a snack. I remember that my mother always had one or two large cold rhubarb tarts on the table.

The pleasure part of the fair was held, as now, on the opposite side of the road. The roundabouts were smaller than now and owned by a Mrs Brett. These were worked by an old pony that used to trot round, while the organ was turned by a boy and there was no platform underneath the horses.

One of the stalls that were always at the fair was the "Sausage Stall" run by an old woman who sold hot sausages at a ha'penny each. Another was a cake stall run by old Mr Garner of Aylesbury. My mother would always buy some of his "Banbury Cakes".

In those days Coconut shies had their nuts places in cups and not rammed into sockets as they do now, and the game known as "Touch 'Em" used wooden pins instead of iron ones. Mention of the game called "Touch 'Em" brings back to my mind an incident that happened years later. I have often told this story, but I think I'll tell it again.

The first time that the fair people introduced the iron pins to Wendover, some of the usual customers – mainly the boys from off the hills who could really throw straight – became rather annoyed. One of these "up hill" boys named Harry Chandler from Swan Bottom, was apprenticed to my father and when evening came, he and I went out to the fair. Harry could throw as straight as a gun shot and with terrific speed. To give some idea of his prowess, I have seen him throw an addled hen's egg right over a very high old elm tree. Well as usual we visited a "Touch 'Em" stall but try how he would the iron pins would not fall over.

It so happened that we had in the wood shop a round piece of meteorite or thunderbolt. It was the same size as the showman's wooden balls and very heavy. This gave Harry Chandler an idea; we fetched this lump of meteorite and returned to the stall. Harry bought three more balls, a penny for three, and threw two; then let fly with the "Hell's Clinker" as we called it. This hit one of the pins, broke the top off it and went straight though the canvas at the back. In accordance with pre-arranged agreement, both of us grabbed as many packets of cigarettes as we could and ran like mad. I shall never forget the look of utter bewilderment on the face of the showman as he saw what he thought was a wooden ball go through the canvas. We never saw our Hell's Clinker again, perhaps the showman found it.

I well remember the first time that steam roundabouts were used in the street. It was at a May Fair. I had been ill so I could not go out, but the steam roundabout proprietor, a man named Wall from Thame, came to my father asking if he could erect his roundabouts in front of the old shop, as Mrs Brett had already set hers up in the usual place. My father agreed and I was delighted to watch them building the roundabouts up close to the window. Mr Wall had almost finished when along came the police and moved him off because he was obstructing the footpath. In consequence of this Mr Wall moved his roundabouts to a site opposite Thompson's shop and I remember my bitter disappointment.

Not long after this Mrs Brett went out of business and that was the end of pony-driven roundabouts at Wendover fair as Mr Wall took over and very soon became the owner of a set of Galloping Horses. He carried on for a few years until two other firms pushed him out. These were Wilsons and Smith and Whittle. The latter used to travel with a complete fair and usually held the fair in the Kings Head orchard. Wilsons usually held theirs in Wharf Meadow.

Many people nowadays try to condemn the fair being held in the street and would abolish it if they could but Wendover Fair dates back to the days of Queen Elizabeth when it received its charter and cannot be abolished with just a wave of the hand. Perhaps all this talk about Wendover Fair may seem somewhat pointless and not very interesting, but remember, reader, that this book is written to recall the memories of Wendover as I knew it and to try to convey just what these events meant to the people of all ages in those days.

Wheelwrights, Watering Cans and Witchell

Another outstanding event was the annual Flower Show, always held in those days on August Tuesday, in the Manor House Park. Besides the usual show of flowers, fruit, vegetables, etc., there was a cricket match and sports of one kind or another, as well as outdoor concerts or competitions. I well remember watching a "Sticky Bun Competition" but was not allowed to compete.

During the South African War, I cannot remember the exact year, but think it must have been about 1900, a mouth organ playing competition was staged. The judge was Rev. C. E. Roberts, rector of Halton, who was a very fine musician and kept a private school at The Chilterns, and the prizes consisting of new mouth organs were given by Mr E J Sharp. I could always play one of these instruments, so I was allowed to enter. I played the then very popular Kipling Song "The Absent Minded Beggar", which was a patriotic song written to suit the sentiments of the Boer War, and was delighted to be awarded second prize. The old mouth organ won on the day is still knocking around and will still play.

The annual Flower Show was also the means of letting a good many Wendover people not only see a motor car for the first time but also to ride in one. The vehicle was more like an old-time two-horse pleasure brake body on a car chassis and held about six or eight people sitting face to face. It ran to and from the show ground, fetching and carrying people at sixpence per head. My father, mother and grandmother all had a ride and of course they took me with them.

A show committee man rode in the front with the driver to collect the fares. On the occasion on which I rode, the committee man was the late Mr Albert Payne, father of Mrs Dean, and who used to keep the shop in London Road as a rope, string and sack shop. We got on the motor car as it came down from the show ground and rode down as far as the Temperance Hotel to pick up the rest of the load and then on to the show. Everybody was excited and perhaps a bit afraid. Goodness knows what people would think of having a ride in a similar contraption nowadays.

Speaking of shows, I can also remember the Wendover and Chiltern Hills Agricultural Show being held in the meadow next to Witchell, and I believe I have some faint recollection of produce being laid somewhere in the Red Lion Yard, but I may be wrong in this. Anyhow these were the forerunners of many very fine agricultural shows held right up to the outbreak of the 1914 war in the part of Halton where the RAF workshops now stand. These shows were great days, a military band was engaged and a military Tournament staged by the Royal Bucks Yeomanry as well as a Jumping and Driving Contest and Tradesmans Turnout Competition. But the main attraction for a great many people were the grounds of Halton House, which were thrown open to the public by Mr Alfred de Rothschild and it was a great treat for music lovers to hear Mr Rothschild's own private band playing in the grounds.

The coronation of King Edward VII was another day that lives in the memory of many. Following a service at the Parish Church the people of Wendover went to Halton Park where, with the people of Weston Turville, they were the guests of Mr Alfred de Rothschild. I well remember going, and the spread that we had. About this time there was a travelling theatrical company running their own show in a fair-sized building of wood and canvas in the meadow opposite the King and Queen and they was engaged to give performances. I remember my mother taking me into the big marquee erected for the occasion to see "Charlie's Aunt" and whenever I hear of this play, the memory of that day at Halton springs up.

There were two bands, Wendover Pipe Band and Weston Turville band and in the evening a great Bonfire was lit on "Old Knoll". Speaking of bonfires on Old Knoll, recalls another occasion, that of the peace celebrations at the end of the Boer War. I remember this so well as I was scared to death by the rockets, the first I ever saw.

Two other days of rejoicing and flag decorations were the relief of Mafeking and Ladysmith as were also the various days when the Wendover men returned from the War. They were usually met at the station by the band and the fire brigade and were pulled on the fire engine to a platform, erected near where the War Memorial now stands, to be publicly welcomed and presented with an illuminated address. When the vicar's son, Capt (later Major) Edwin Smith returned, I was one of the schoolchildren who sang a song of welcome under the direction of the schoolmaster.

Returning to festivities at Halton Park, the coronation of King George V was celebrated in much the same way as that of Edward VII but this time I was one of those who played in the Wendover Band and received a pipe and an ounce of tobacco.

As darkness fell a wonderful thing for those days happened. An open air cinema show of the coronation procession was given. This may sound very ordinary nowadays, but it was a revelation then.

A large bonfire was built on Old Knoll but, alas, someone lit it before the appointed time.

i Joseph Floyd, as a young man

ii Harry Floyd, with his watering can!

iii Alice Lavinia Floyd

iv The King's Head, High Street

v The Two Brewers

vi London Road, also called South Street

vii Aylesbury Street. The Fire Station is on the right

viii The Station Bridge

ix Florence Floyd (neé Thompson)
Wife of Harry, Mother of Wilf and
Oliver, Grandmother of Diana

x Joseph Floyd

xi The funeral of the cub scout. Harry Floyd leading

xii Betty, Wilf and Oliver blowing bubbles in
the back garden of 29 High Street

xiii Harry and Florence Floyd
in the 1940s

xiv Freeman's at the top of the High Street

xv Oliver and Diana Floyd at a fete in Hale Road

xvi Diana in paddling pool at 27 Hampden Road

xvii Diana's birthday at 27 Hampden Road. Diana is fourth from the left

xviii Diana's birthday party at Twin Wells. Back row l-r: unknown, Joanne Thomas, Diana Floyd, Jenny and Sally. Front l-r: Frances Dunnett, Guy Niblett, Zoe Didsbury and Sharn.

xix Diana c 1964 as Telstar

xx Barbara Floyd planting a Whitebeam to the memory of her husband, Oliver in March 1980. Mike, Diana and Gavin are far right. Jack Floyd is seventh from left, next to Cicely Webb, Diana's godmother. The others are friends, relatives and members of the parish council. The tree is flourishing in Witchell.

Chapter 13

The Monastery and Burnt Hands

When I started to write this book it was really meant to be a record of what I remember during my life, but as I have often strayed into items of interest that took place before my time and description of places in Wendover that have been explained to me by old people I may as well add something that may be of interest to others at some future date. But before going on it may be as well to relate just why I started to write at all. I have spent many happy hours sitting by the fireside with my children, telling them stories of my childhood days and it occurred to me that they may like to recall some of these some day so I decided to put them on paper.

Now to return to more anecdotes. I cannot write this book without some reference to our dear old Parish Church and some of its surroundings; everyone knows where the Vicarage stands but how many people know where the old Vicarage was? According to the old men mentioned earlier on, it stood at the south side of the church in the grounds of the present Manor House, roughly halfway between the Manor House and the Church. A coach drive ran down through the church yard, entering the road at the top of Church Hill. This can still be seen by an indentation in the bank on the road side. The coach road was lined with trees, some of which still stand along the path in the church yard.

The portion of ground taken into the churchyard after the 1914-18 war, where the tool shed stands, was where the coach road was, and was supposed to have never been included in the church yard at all before and had certainly never been used as a burial ground.

It so happened that for some time after the First World War Wendover had no sexton or grave digger and undertakers had to arrange for graves to be dug themselves. My father used to undertake funerals so it often fell to my lot to assist in grave digging and it so happened that Harry Chandler and I had to dig one of the first graves ever opened on that particular piece of ground.

This grave had to be dug deep enough for three people and after digging through about eighteen inches of the old coach road we struck the chalky soil. On reaching the depth of about 6ft 6in we suddenly came upon a human skeleton, we had actually opened up an ancient grave because the skull was exactly at the head of the new grave and the feet at the bottom. Thinking that we had been opening new ground, this was something of a shock, so we left digging and I went to see Mr W J Stevens who was Church warden at the time, as I thought the discovery might be of some interest. He was astounded and we searched the old records but they only appeared to prove that the piece of ground was virgin soil as far as regards burials. Anyway, he accompanied me to the churchyard and saw for himself but still claimed that it was jut a chance discovery of human remains.

Soon after this we had to dig another deep grave at the head of the first one and there we found another skeleton. This happened on several other occasions and each one was exactly on the spot of a previous grave, proving beyond doubt that this piece of ground had been a burial ground long before the records of the church were kept or the coach road built. I still have two pieces of ivory, like large animals teeth, dug from the first grave.

During the time that Rev Cornibeer was vicar of Wendover, a gentleman who is an authority on churches visited him and concluded that at some time in the past, the south door of the church was the main entrance owing the ancient porch. If this was really so, the discovery just related would appear to be more likely to fit into the general picture.

In passing, it has been proved that of all the old Yew trees around the church, the one at the Belfry end is the oldest. I wonder how many babies that tree has see carried into the church to be christened, and then carried in as old people for their burial. Morbid thought did you say, reader? Well, maybe, but it does no harm to halt for a moment in this hurrying world and think.

The Parish Church has and always will hold lovely memories for me as well as a few sad ones. As far back as I remember, my father sang in the choir. This he did for sixteen years, leaving in 1909. Then a year later I took his place and served for 29 years, during which time I had seen my own two sons join as choirboys.

While on the subject of the church it may not be out of place to write something here on one of the oldest buildings in Wendover. I mean the Post Office and Bosworth House. These houses are the remains or at least, parts of the remains of an ancient monastery, which was once a branch of the monastic body of Southwark. The only real relic of this monastery still to be seen is a curiously shaped stone thing just inside the large gateway. There has been much controversy as to what it really is, but the late Mr Fred Mead, who used to live there before the house became a Post Office, claimed that it was a font. I have learned much in more recent years about this queer stone thing and the buildings around it which is, to say the least, very interesting, but whatever it may be, I have seen Sisters of Mercy visit the place on many occasions, bow before it and stand for a few moments as if in an attitude of prayer.

Wheelwrights, Watering Cans and Witchell

I have just claimed to have learned a lot about the old monastery in recent years. The question that will naturally spring to the reader's mind is "How?" It was this way. After returning from the Great War in 1919, I used to think very deeply about my friends who would never come home, and, as was the case with thousands of others, my early religious teachings would not satisfy me. I therefore began a study of the world's religions to find the answer and after years of study and search I found the only train of thought that would give me the answer I sought, and so it was that I began to study Spiritualism, and it has been through this channel that I have learned about the old monastery.

I here assert that I have talked to the Father Abbot of the Monastery and this is what he told those who were met together on one occasion.

The monastic buildings stretched from and included, Bosworth House to the *Kings Head*. The most holy part or chapel was at the site of the present kitchen and gateway and the curious stone thing was not a font but a piscina. The monastery proper was on the upper side of the gateway and what is now Bell's shop was the guest house. He also said that the Father Abbot's house was on the other side of the road where the "house with two wells" now stands. Curiously enough, Freemans shop has two wells inside and is called "Two Wells" by the present owner.

There is much more I could write but I think that is enough. I can quite imagine the reader giving a rather scoffing laugh, but wait, when Mr Fred Wood repaired the interior of Bosworth House, some very old paintings were found on the walls, one of these painting is now in the British Museum. Mr Wood already knew of the presence of the pictures on the walls The Father Abbot had told him. I was there when he did so.

Before leaving the monastery there is one other thing. A few years ago, Mr Carter discovered a small cement floor in his garden when digging a celery trench, it was so hard that nothing would break it. A gentleman from the British Museum saw this floor and declared it to be a kiln floor which had at one time been a monastery brewery. He was told about the old monastery across the road and came to the conclusion that the origin of "Witchell" and "Hollands" ponds was probably as fish ponds to supply the monks with their Friday fish.

Mr F. W. Blake claims to be something of an authority on Wendover and its ancient history and has written a book on it. I have discussed the details regarding the monastery with him, but of course, being a strictly orthodox man he refuses to accept those things that I have chronicled here. I don't really blame him, I should probably have done the same at one time, but after more than 16 years of study of Spiritualism, I know better.

Well I seem to be getting ahead of myself a bit so must return to the year 1900.

The Boer War was at its height but unlike the two World Wars it did not affect the people in England to any great degree. Naturally, those who had relatives in South Africa in the Forces were anxious and those who were left to look after the businesses of the soldiers had a worrying time but there were no irritating restrictions, no rationing or queues and of course no blackout. Aeroplanes were unknown, although the Army did use captive balloons for observation purposes; the round type of balloon with a basket underneath, as pictures in the periodicals of those days will prove. Of course there was no such things as wireless and all messages or reports came by either cable or sea. I well remember how people used to send some of the letters received from their friends and relatives in the Forces, to the Bucks papers for publication and how attentively I used to listen to my mother reading them.

It was in the spring of 1900 that plans were started for the making up of my father's new yard and the removal of old shops and building new ones in their present position. Up to that date, the two gardens of Bosworth and Floyd Houses joined about on the centre of the present roadway, while the part now occupied by the yard was a fruit orchard.

I did not see the actual building of the new shops or the demolition of the old ones which was completed in the month of June, because I was one of a few unlucky Wendover children who contracted a form of fever which was thought to have been brought by the caravan children who came to the May Fair, but it was a great thrill to see it all when I got about again.

Up to this time all my father's ironwork had been done by Mr Carter at the forge across the road, but Mr Carter had gone to the War with the Royal Engineers and an old, one-eyed man named Tom Putman was running the business. Putman became rather officious and refused to do some of the smaller jobs when they were needed. This got on my father's nerves and in 1901 he decided to build a forge and do his own ironwork, that is how the forge now used by Mr F Birch came into being.

Speaking of the old man Putman, brings to my mind how cruel many of those older men were to the boys of my day. One day I saw a queer-shaped piece of iron lying at the anvil block in Carter's shop and speaking about it to old Putman. He at once told me to pick it up and take it away. I was only about eight years old and was very pleased to be given this small piece of iron, but on picking it up discovered that it was very hot, the red heat only just having died down. It burnt the skin off my fingers and thumb to the intense delight of Putman. Another trick played on the farm boys who took

Wheelwrights, Watering Cans and Witchell

horses to be shod at Caudreys was to "unlock the brains". This was delighted in by Ben Ratcliffe who would force a small key up the boys' nose and turn it. These were only two examples of cruelty but one old man mentioned earlier on, Jim Dancer, always rejoiced to say that he always hit a boy when he saw him because, "if he did not deserve it, then he would in a few minutes".

The boys of today may still deserve a hiding now and again but it is a good thing these ideas held by old men have died out. I have known many boys who were scared stiff to let their fathers know that they had had the cane at school in case they got another good cut "to keep it company" and believe me that was definitely unnecessary after one of Mr Bushell's "specials".

The writings of Harry Floyd end here. The last chapter was written shortly before his death in 1947 at the age of 54.

Wilf Floyd

Chapter 14

Harry Thomas Floyd

Harry covered some events of his childhood but got little further, so this chapter covers aspects of later life and his involvement in Wendover organisations. As he said, a great deal of his early years were spent at Church Farm, Little Kimble. It is obvious that he regarded this part of Little Kimble as one of the most beautiful parts of Bucks, and his deep affection for his Rayner grandparents is very much in evidence. The Rayner family were native to that area and a number of their graves can be seen in Ellesborough churchyard.

On leaving school Harry Floyd joined the business and was apprenticed in London to learn the signwriting trade. In 1915 he joined the army and his RAMC unit was stationed at Halton Camp initially so it must have seemed a lucky posting, because during some weekends and leave he was able to do some painting jobs for the business.

The YMCA, based at Wendover School, was also a useful stopping-off point. He went to France in early 1918 and saw some action in the ensuing year. He kept a personal diary throughout his army service. An entry for 4 November 1918, just one week before the armistice reads: "Moved up with Padre into the front line. Barrage opened at six o'clock. Went 'over' with Batt. Shall never forget it. How I prayed." A casual entry one week later reads: "Full day off. Laid about and read. Armistice from 11.30." No sign there of any burst of relief or enthusiasm for the end of the bloodiest of wars but perhaps he reflected the general caution or weariness of the time among the troops. He was demobilised in 1919 and in June of that year married Florence Thompson in her village church at Hever, Kent.

Returning to the business, he also became involved again in Wendover organisations. The Wendover Branch of the Discharged and Demobilised Sailors and Soldiers Federation was active and held concerts and as a solo tenor he sang at other village concerts. He was also secretary of the Wendover Floral and Horticultural Association and the Prime Minister of the day was a subscriber to this body. Prime Ministers connections in this activity arose I think from their Chequers residence and were still maintained to the time of Ramsey McDonald.

Then there was the local Boys Brigade in which he headed the Ambulance Section. Scouting also took up some time and he became Group Scoutmaster in the late 1920s and later was appointed District Commissioner. In the 1930s he was a member of the Church Parochial

Council and in local politics he stood for the Parish Council. The Wendover British Legion also saw him as a long-serving committee member and one time treasurer and secretary. In the heydays of the Wendover Football Club he was the trainer and also the editor of the weekly football programme. During all this time he was a regular member of the Parish Church choir and churchgoer, and was tenor soloist in many of the church productions. So all in all it is a bit of an understatement to say that he played an active part in the social events of the town!

This chapter would not be complete without a word or two on his connection with Spiritualism, of which he make some mention in his memoirs. Apart from home circles, he used to occasionally go to the Post Office a couple of doors away where the switchboard operator at that time was a natural, if reluctant, trance medium named Wilfred Lovegrove who was, incidentally, organist at St John's Catholic church in Aylesbury. Sessions held there were the source of his comments about Bosworth House. He kept this part of his life away from us children, and as a young teenager my recollection is only of using the magazine 'Greater World' as sturdy shinpads when I played football. They were solid and saved a few leg injuries!

Later on, at my request, I accompanied him to the Aylesbury church to learn something of the subject. He used to conduct healing services once a week and became vice-president of the church. Very late in his life he developed into a trance medium but so far as I am aware he gave no public demonstrations of this at the Spiritualist Church. It's not my intention in this record to argue the pros and cons of this subject. I would only say that I am convinced that self delusion played no part whatever in these events, and certainly there was no money in it, as is sometimes claimed by sceptics.

When the wheelwrights business collapsed in the 1930s he turned his hand to any manual or clerical job available at the time, and they were hard times. He joined the War Reserve Constabulary but was not too highly thought of by the 'professionals' because the number of cases he booked was a bit below par! He was always reluctant to bring charges for petty offences such as those committed by cyclists and this reflected in the numbers game that was one benchmark of police efficiency.

The reader of Harry Floyd's memoirs may conclude that he was slightly deferential towards the landed gentry of the early part of the 20th century, such as the Lord of the Manor. I don't think this was so, but it probably says something of the forelock-touching attitudes of that era. The paternalistic approach of such people must undoubtedly have had a beneficial effect on the Wendover community, and improved their quality of life. But the people

Wheelwrights, Watering Cans and Witchell

who contributed most to the fabric of the whole community were the ordinary 'doers'; contemporaries such as Basil Purssell, Harry Benning, Joe Holland, and others whose names appear in The New History of Wendover, published in 1972. Harry Floyd may be numbered among these folk. His health began to fail during the 1940s due to deteriorating kidneys and he died of kidney failure at the age of 54 in 1947, medical advancements of today being unavailable.

He is buried in Wendover churchyard, together with his wife.

Chapter 15

Florence Floyd

A few words now about my mother, Florence Floyd. She was born at Grantham in 1890, her father being John Thompson. He was a butler who, during the Edwardian era, served some time at Hever Castle, Kent with the Astor family. He and his wife moved to Wendover on retirement and lived in Sydney Terrace. They also lived in a cottage next to Ellesborough Church for a while and it is a mark of people's energy in the 1920s that my mother used to regularly push me in a pram from Wendover to visit them and think nothing of it.

She had spent her early life in and around Hever, and following a spell as a children's nurse she moved to Wendover after her marriage in 1919. She was at one time engaged to an Edgar Harrington from Edenbridge, and he enlisted for the Great War. He was killed at the front in 1917. She received a card from Edgar dated 30 July 1917 to say he was quite well. She did not hear from him again, and a letter from the War Office stated that he was posted missing on 31 July, one day later. She kept these papers and although this attachment in no way detracted from her devotion to Harry Floyd, the name of Edgar often cropped up in home conversation.

She was a devoted wife and mother and led a very hard life coping with a growing family during the lean 1930s and family illness in the 1940s. As one might imagine, she needed to be very supportive of my father's activities over this period, a period in which family income was at a very low level. There were never any holidays, summer or winter, and odd shoes and make-do clothing were not uncommon for us children. I should say that other children suffered similar deprivations in those depression days but it did not impair the close family life and sense of humour.

We enjoyed ourselves in a variety of improvised ways. Florence was an active member of the Mothers Union and Womens' Institute and she devoted a lot of time to the British Legion Womens' Section, being secretary for a number of years. She was also the Standard Bearer and was made a life member of the Legion in the 1960s. She was a reluctant pensioner and during her 60s used to help at old folks' functions rather than participate, although in later years she had a very full diary of social events among the senior citizens as other younger Wendover ladies took up the voluntary torch. She died at the age of 83 in 1974 and is buried with her husband in Wendover churchyard.

Chapter 16

Coachbuilding between the Wars

The coachbuilding and wheelwrights premises at the end of Floyd's Yard consisted of several large sheds or 'shops'. One paint shop was for the application of undercoats and the making and stitching of canvas hoods and celluloid windows for the cars of the 1920s. Another paint shop, kept protected as much as possible against dust, was used for finishing and finework. A wood shop was used for a variety of manufactures such as cart wheels and also coffins. Two open wood sheds were used for storing the large rough elm and oak planks for seasoning. Then there was the blacksmiths shop nearby for making the iron work for carts including the hoops for cart wheels, as well as the farrier trade. On the open ground between the sheds was the circular cement base to which a cart wheel was fixed for the burning on of the iron rim. A fire would be lit to heat the hoop which would then be fitted and doused with water.

As can be imagined, the nature of the business had to live with change during the late 1920s as motorised trade began to overtake the horse drawn wagons and eventually, of course, it had to give way completely and the automated processes of the garages took over. In the early years of change however, the labour-intensive methods of the coachbuilder were still applied to cars of the day, such as the decorative gold lining and hand-painted lettering. Books of thin gold leaf were very precious and were used to the last scrap. A small book of gold leaf would cost about ten shillings, which represented about a quarter of a week's wages. In the busy days there would be several carts, etc., parked awaiting some sort of treatment, and horses tethered awaiting shoeing.

The doors of the main paint shop were covered in paint to a depth of about a quarter of an inch, from the colour testing. Paint was mixed from solid blocks that were ground in a fairly small but heavy iron paint mill. I gave this mill, one of my father's treasured possessions, to the Aylesbury Museum and hopefully it is still displayed as one of the old trades implements. Paint-spraying was accomplished with a manually-operated pump. The wood shop contained a large band saw and drills and these were precariously wedged between the beams. There is no way that they would have been acceptable under the health and safety regulations of the current day, particularly bearing in mind the hours that we young children would spend playing with them and swinging on them. There were never any bad injuries though, but one might attribute this to sheer good fortune.

Apart from work on the premises, signwriting and inn sign painting jobs were carried on in the town, and this work normally fell to my father. Tree felling in the local fields, principally Witchell, helped to replenish the timber stocks.

Much of this timber was used for making coffins, as part of the undertaking trade that was part of the business. Rich clients had oak coffins while others had elm. All were beautifully made and lined, and it was the habit of many folk in those days to store a new night dress or gown especially for use at their burial.

The blacksmith was Freddie Birch, a wiry man only about five foot tall but capable of controlling the largest of the shire horses that had to be shod. He lived in Chandos Alley (later upgraded to Chandos Place) that ran off Back Street, although this row of cottages was demolished in the 1960s to make way for housing development. He was invariably jovial and sang at the top of his voice while shoeing, usually hymns. His repertoire included 'Jesus wants me for a sunbeam', 'I wonder will the angels sing up yonder', and 'Oh that I had the wings of angels'. When a particularly nervous horse was giving him trouble, he would whack it in the belly with his large hammer and shout "Stand still yer bugger", and then return to his singing. Freddie continued his trade for some years after the coachbuilding business folded, and he died at a ripe old age in the 1970s.

By 1930 the first signs of declining fortunes started to emerge, as evidenced by cryptic diary entries:

2 Nov 1929	Had to stand Lionel off due to slack trade.
7 Sept 1930	Anxiety still tense but hoping something will turn up before long. No work to look forward to.
1 Oct 1932	Terrible workless week.
5 Oct 1932	Work came in.

When work came in it was usually a busy period to meet timescales. My father would snatch a quick cup of tea before returning to the task, and it was at these times that we were taught the rudiments of etiquette. One should never blow on tea to cool it, we were told, you should always fan it with your cap!

This patchwork existence continued into the mid 1930s when eventually he had to call it a day. During this period, life for all of us was extremely frugal because there were no sources of public support available. These were the depression years with a vengeance although somehow the situation never registered with us children who were quite happy with our lot, and the yard became an exciting playground. Guy Fawkes nights were particularly exciting as they provided an opportunity to get rid of old tyres and other accumulated rubbish, and neighbours and friends were invited.

Harry turned his skills to a number of jobs as they turned up, having left the ranks of the self-employed, and a diary entry in 1938 records...

> 6 May 1938   My biggest pay day - £4.3s.9d Great jubilation.

During all this period however, our parents managed to see all three of us children to secondary schools, my sister and I to Aylesbury Grammar and my brother to High Wycombe Technical. Scholarships helped of course, but the support was never lacking.

So ended the Floyd business and perhaps the last of the old trades in Wendover at that time. Just the name "Floyd's Yard" remains, in spirit if not in fact.

Chapter 17

Wendover School

It is to the credit of the architects and planners that the shell of the old Wendover C of E schools has been maintained, following its conversion to living accommodation in the 1960s.

The quality of teaching in the 1920s and 1930s is, I suppose, a matter for each individual to express, but the school had its usual crop of 'characters' and much of the teaching involved parrot fashion chanting, or so it seems with hindsight. In some cases, such as tables, it is perhaps as good a method as any but maybe it was carried a bit far. Statistically, the school probably rated on a par with other surrounding villages in scholarship success rates.

Teachers in those days were two Miss Burnetts, Miss 'Tiger' Eldridge, Miss Smith, Miss Dawson, Miss Irving, and at the top class, Tom Sears. Each had their own styles of course. Successive headmasters were Mr Mollineux, Mr Jones, Mr Morris and Mr Burgess. A fiery teacher in the 30s was a young Miss Jones who was not beyond flinging a tuning fork at any misbehaving child. There is, or was, a tree lined lane running from Heron Path (opposite Chapel Lane) into Hale Road called Dark Lane, and a familiar boys' school rhyme ran "Up Dark Lane where nobody goes, see Gert Jones without any clothes" Ah well, boys will be boys, and all in all Miss Jones commanded respect.

Schooling was punctuated by occasional religious holidays such as Ascension Day when a church parade in the morning was followed by a half-day holiday. Visits to the school by the school dentist were treated with some apprehension as treatment was rushed and rather callous. Another visitor was the 'Head' doctor who examined for lice and the system was a bit divisive because those with lice were set to one side for the others to see. It put a bit of a stigma on them and you always knew who to avoid and to jeer at.

The ponds and stream in Witchell were a good source of animal life such as tadpoles for school interest and education and some lucky pupils (myself included) would be nominated on a Friday afternoon to go up to Witchell to change the water in the fish bowls. Digressing for a moment, another rich source of pond life was Hampden Pond near the church, a breeding place for frogs and toads. These animals had a lemming like instinct to migrate from the pond across the London Road towards the allotments and railway line beyond. Many made it, but very many more did not, and the road was littered with their squashed bodies from the passing traffic. On a hot summer's day the stench in this area was quite an experience.

School bullies and the like were very much as they are today I suppose, though perhaps without some of the vicious vandalism. Horace Wheatley was a boy who always wore hob-nailed boots and delighted in stamping on anyone wearing soft shoes, but he himself was not without his tormentors. Pastimes used to have their appointed seasons, such a whipping tops in the spring, followed by percussion cap loaded keys for throwing at the wall or the ground in the summer, then googly balls which were unevenly weighted rubber balls popular in the 30s, and cigarette card throwing where the winner could build up a good collection. Marbles were very popular as well and the roadside gutters offered a good playing area for this activity. Conkers of course left the playground littered with debris in the autumn.

In the school holidays the 'trackers' came out, the simplest being a board fixed to four pram wheels, and the more elaborate had a box seat and a brake. The gentler slopes of the hills tested the skills and the durability of both driver and vehicle and of course brought the usual crop of minor injuries.

One national sporting event that seemed to whip up more enthusiasm than the FA Cup Final was the Boat Race. For weeks beforehand the sweet shops would be offering dark blue and light blue gobstoppers and feathered emblems to display on jumpers and jackets according to one's choice. Picking sides for playground games was made easier! The days at the old school had plenty of variety.

Chapter 18

Social Events in Wendover

The Public Hall, a wooden structure in Aylesbury Road later given over to housing development, was the venue for most indoor events such as concerts, children's' parties, boxing tournaments, etc., and could always boast a good attendance. Outdoor fetes and celebrations such as Jubilee and Coronation always seemed to have one thing in common – the fancy dress parades. These were always very popular and usually entailed a procession around a designated route through the town before arriving at the fete grounds. Competition was quite fierce. For example in a Hospital Carnival in 1923 my sister was in a pram pushed by her Aunt Margaret and was starved of food all morning. She was given liberal jam sandwiches just before the judging and this achieved the desired result of a well jam covered face that won them a prize as a gypsy couple!

Our family always seemed to get involved in these competitions. My father used to be a good improviser in this activity and won several prizes. One last-minute idea was at the George VI Coronation when he entered as a policeman with Freddie Birch as 'The man who burned the bonfire' - it had been lit a couple of nights before by persons unknown. They won first prize.

The main weekly or fortnightly attraction for the dedicated was the Football Club, and the mid 1930s saw Wendover reach its peak in this sphere as members of the Spartan League, capable of taking on and beating local rivals Aylesbury. Bryants Acre was the venue, and the changing hut was wired for Tannoy music, etc. The weekly programmes, which were sold in good number, were edited by Harry Floyd who was also the trainer. His home-brewed linament, a mixture of camphor and other oils with vinegar and eggs was pungent and seem to do the trick! The crowd, and the players, were no angels even in those days, and any player of the opposing team who got in the way of Mrs Edmond's umbrella knew what it was all about. The most keenly fought matches were in the Oving Village Cup however, and I imagine that this is still the case, although the standard of football in Wendover has never reached these heights again.

'Teenie' Wells was a short but very capable goalkeeper and other local names that were well represented on the field were from the Edmonds, Simmons and Swain families.

Of course, as previously mentioned in this record, the Fair was a great attraction, although by this time the sheep and cattle side had disappeared.

Wheelwrights, Watering Cans and Witchell

The large and brightly polished traction engines provided much of the power and lighting, supplemented by napthamene flare lamps and the Pettigrove family held sway. Old Mrs Pettigrove sat in her caravan near the big roundabouts and would carefully count all the riding customers to make sure that her sons were not fiddling her as they collected the fares. One stall that we used to watch opposite our house was the sweet stall, when they were making mint rock. The mixture would be repeatedly flung over hooks and pulled and twisted. The only snag was that the puller used to get a better grip by spitting on the hands! Whether this improved the taste I'll never know, because we kept well away from that treat.

Water squirters, small lead tubes filled with water, were always popular and added immensely to all the debris that was left after the fair. Searching through all this debris for 'goodies' was quite productive. The second world war really put paid to the novelty of the fair which never achieved its old momentum. During the war a single Roll-a-Penny stall would sometimes be the only attraction, and was sent purely to maintain the continuity required by the ancient charter.

The picturesque scene of the brightly painted, spic and span Romany caravans parked up Dobbins Lane as far as the tennis courts, was replaced by the motorised units common today.

Chapter 19

Religious Life and Wendover Church

Probably the biggest contrast with life of today is seen in the attitudes to religious and church affairs, and although Wendover is no different from elsewhere in this respect, it's a good example.

Sundays were quiet and observed days when, even in the 1930's and except for the occasional sweet shop, there was little else obtainable. On special days of course items could be bought, such as fresh hot cross buns from Thompson's bakery on Good Friday, or figs on Palm (or Fig) Sunday. The inevitable locked church of today has to be compared with the free access available at all times.

Funerals were often very solemn and staged events, with a slow procession of vehicles wending its way up the High Street and along London Road to the church. The convoy would be headed by a walking escort of six bearers dressed in funeral attire and well brushed tall black hats. They were often led by my father as part of his undertaking commitments. Curtains would be drawn in the house windows as a mark of respect. One of the plates shows a procession in the 1920s when a young cub scout had been killed by a car in Aylesbury road. This was a boy named Norman Ray (his father was Wendover Station Master), and for many years a statue of a cub could be seen in the churchyard on his grave Unfortunately it's now in pieces. The procession is led by my father as scoutmaster (see plate xi).

Sunday walks to and from the church were quite a ritual, with raised hats and 'good mornings' to the large-hatted ladies, most of whom one only met on Sundays. I joined the choir at about eight years old but had to sit near the organist behind the choir, to learn the drill. The organ bellows had to be pumped by whoever was available. Later, as a server as well as a choir boy, it was not unusual to attend four services in the day to carry out the duties so it was a pretty full day. Choirboys used to get a penny per service. There was normally a pretty good attendance at all services, and it was quite an art to estimate the number of likely communicants for the wine in the chalice. One vicar, who shall be nameless, frequently used to overestimate and as all the wine had to be consumed, he had to empty the cup!

Probably the most memorable occasion was the Armistice Day evening parade, when the church was full to bursting. The procession was led through Wendover, first to the war memorial and then to the church, by the full RAF band from Halton. The return procession took the same form. This procession still takes place of course on Remembrance Sunday, but the intensity and emotions of the community on 11 November with their memories of the then fairly recent war could not possibly be matched today.

The bell-ringers of the day were an enthusiastic lot. They were led as I recall by Abel Rance, but the tenor bell was rung by Joe Hopcraft, a short but stocky gentleman who revelled in going up with the rope and landing with a thump as he came down. We could hear this thump from the vestry above the noise of the bells.

At the outbreak of the Second World War the vicar, John Lister, broke into the morning service to announce Chamberlain's broadcast, and once again the war seemed to be a benchmark in the church's future, and in church attendance and attitudes. The evening service in the winters of World War Two was at 3pm to avoid the blackout hours and was held in dim candle light and a few muted lamps.

My father had a good rapport with the vicars of the day, except John Lister. He was an ex-army Chaplain with the brusque manner of a man more used to relating to military personnel than to the mixed community of a small town. He very rarely composed the sermon, preferring instead to read from sometimes long and boring pastoral communiques. His services also tended to take on a rather rushed and 'Let's get it over with' style. He alienated a lot of people including my father and brother who left the local church. I stayed on for a while, still tinkling the communion bell, or swinging the incense that he had introduced to some rare services, but eventually other activities and then National Service put paid to that.

Chapter 20

Changing Face of Wendover

This record has attempted to trace a little of the evolution of the town from the late 1800s.

Before the Enclosures Act of 1796 some parts of the centre had already been enclosed, with gardens and paddocks near the houses which enabled the farmers to house the livestock that they did not wish to keep on the common lands such as The Clay and Malm Fields that extended towards Bottendon (Boddington) Hill. At that time, the populated areas included High Street, Pound Street, London Road as far as Witchell, Aylesbury Street as far as Wharf Road, and Tring Road up to Clay Lane, together with a few buildings near the Church. High Street and Back Street appeared to be one main road with buildings down the middle, including the old Market Hall.

Many houses would have been small farm houses with wide stable doors through with the animals could pass to the farmyard beyond. By the mid 1800s the farms in the centre were disappearing and, as indicated in these records, by the late 1800s had given way to some of the supporting trades. The population on the other hand which had risen by about 40 percent in the thirty years up to 1830, remained static after that and was two thousand in 1900. Then the railway and other improved communications started to take effect.

The gradual change from an essentially farming community to the commuter belt town has been inevitable and sensible but one has to reflect on the losses to the environment as well as the gains. Many of the fields and adventure areas available to the growing children in the 1930s have disappeared, and amusement halls, controlled play areas, and the like, however well planned, are no real substitute. Ironically, the newcomers to Wendover have probably contributed more to the environmental protection of the town that the natives, organising various protection societies. This is a fairly common attitude in any migration, I imagine, where a settler appreciates the place as he selected it and says 'Now that I'm here – no more!'. But the needs dictate the events. In the 1930s there was Mill Meadow in Dobbins Lane, the extensive fields of Cold Comfort stretching towards Worlds End, Bryants Acre, Lower Witchell with its ponds, and the fields up Tring Road. All are now built on and the expansion will no doubt continue.

Some change occurs naturally of course, and the Wendover hills bear some evidence of this. There used to be a steep chalk pit near the foot of the hills, a quite dangerous, steep pit caused by erosion. It's now a gentle grassy slope. Sheep and rabbits controlled the undergrowth and butterflies, especially the chalk blue, were in abundance. Chrysalides of the emerging butterflies were plentiful on the long waving grass. There were the destroyers too, of course, because butterfly nets and birds nesters tended to be encouraged by school teachers rather than forbidden as is now quite rightly the case.

The centre of the town, though, has not changed a very great deal. However there are no longer the Saunders Dairy, the *Kings Head*, Carters and Hibberds Garages, the corner sweet shop at London Road and no-one like Uriah Dell, who used to deliver milk to the door from a milk churn and leave a pot of cream as a Christmas present. A supermarket and a Chinese restaurant reflect the essential need for change and the pace of life.

The locality is cleaner, too, compared with the streets of the 30s, when one could walk down the High Street collecting cigarette cards from the many empty packets thrown into the gutters. The paved Manor Waste has replaced the old rough area, with its remains of an old iron pump beside which one-armed Jim Deering would sit on his 'Stop me and buy one' Walls ice cream tricycle.

Children's behaviour is channelled differently and may be less restrained. That's not to say that there was no vandalism; throwing stones at street lamp bulbs was not uncommon, and when the 'New' recreation ground was opened in the Jubilee year of 1935, it was not many weeks before the glass in the shelter was shattered. But other activities have replaced those such as scrumping and climbing down the railway embankment by the Railway Bridge to put pennies on the line to see them flattened.

Ah well. Nostalgia they say is a thing of the past. So be it – Wendover holds many memories and may it long continue to do so.

POSTSCRIPT

There are no Floyds now in Wendover to my knowledge. We children went our various ways for family or business reasons, and our forebears are long gone.

There is a saying that life is like putting your hand in a bucket of water; when you take it out there is no sign that you were ever there. I don't think this is so: everybody leaves a tiny scratch on the face of history, and one or two of those tiny marks etched on the history of Wendover were made by the people mentioned in this record, and by many not mentioned.

Oliver Floyd

*Recollections of a small town on the Icknield Way
between the Wars*

Foreword

My reasons for writing this I do not intend to qualify. Sufficient to say that I shall enjoy the task, and if only a handful find it an interesting link with the not too distant past, then all will have been worthwhile.

My qualifications for writing such a book, however, I should perhaps establish in more detail. They begin almost a century ago with one, Joseph Floyd, a publican by inheritance and a craftsman by inclination. Members of his family on what must have been his mother's side kept, as the expression goes, the Bear and Cross at Great Kimble, now known as the Bernard Arms, the Inn sign of which explains both names.

I believe, but cannot be certain, that his own father was a publican. What I do know is that Joseph kept *The Bell* in Princes Risborough, and that a rival publican contrived to pull a dirty trick that deprived him of his license. As a result he moved, in 1888, to High Street, Wendover and established himself as Coachbuilder and Wheelwright. At that time he had a wife, Elizabeth and a daughter, Alice Lavinia. Four years later he also had a son, Harry Thomas Floyd. Tragically before the turn of the century, he had only the son.

Several years later he married again, his second wife, a member of the Eldridge family, by whom he had another son, John Francis William, now known to many in Wendover as Jack. Either before or immediately after leaving war service in the RAMC the elder son met and fell for his stepmother's friend, by name Florence Thompson, living in Kent, although born in Grantham of Geordie parents. The couple were married in the little Kent village of Hever in June 1919 and took up residence on the other side of the yard leading to the business which by this time had become Joseph Floyd and Son.

Harry and Florrie had three children. Alice Elizabeth, born 1920, Wilfred Joseph born 1926 and yours truly, conveniently in the middle in 1923. My father was blessed with an excellent memory, which I like to think I have inherited. As a young boy he would apparently sit on a trestle watching his father at work and listening to his fellow trestle-sitters, the very old men of the village who in turn told of what they had listened to in their boyhood days. My father's knowledge of Wendover, therefore, albeit at a mixture at first, second, third or fourth-hand, stretched back to seventeen-something and to hear his recollections was fascinating. He was in the very early stages of committing them to paper when he died in 1947.

Some of his thoughts I could recall for posterity, but will not, and I must make it absolutely clear that the recollections here are entirely mine and owe nothing to anyone else.

They hardly need to. I recall very clearly, if only because the remark hurt me deeply, a schoolteacher saying to me at the age of seven, "You have exactly the same faults when drawing that your father did at your age". Simple calculation indicated that she was talking of teaching him in 1899, so that my second-hand knowledge, without my father's aid, stretches back to last century, whilst my memories begin in the Twenties of this.

To conclude my credentials, I eventually left Wendover in 1969 – although the book refers only to the era that ended just thirty years previously at the outbreak of World War Two. During my adult years I served on the committees of almost every voluntary body, from the Parish Council downwards, with the exception of Women's organisations and the wrong two political parties, so my involvement in Wendover affairs was considerable.

Credentials completed, may I proceed to Chapter One? With one last foreword. Wendover in my time was too large to be considered a village by Buckinghamshire standards, and although hardly qualifying as a town I shall refer to is as that, or as a Parish.

Chapter 21

Along London Road

Wendover, the white river (of chalk) stands on the Icknield Way, the Roman Road from the east and Dunstable, to the west and Wantage.

It is appropriate, however, to approach my Wendover from the direction of London as many a visitor did, by road or the parallel railway – Wendover was one of the most popular destinations for Londoners with cheap day Ramblers' tickets between the wars.

London Road was also the approved route for many of the men and boys who lived outside the parish but worked within it or nearby. The lads from the hills, they were often known as. From Swan Bottom and The Lee on one side, Cobblers Hill and Scrubwood on the other. Strong in the arm were most of these lads, skilled at catching rabbit and game with a stone, and singled out at the twice annual fair as the chaps who smashed the coconuts as they knocked them off.

One of the older of the clan was Billy Burch Snr who for years was boss man at the Sewerage farm (we always knew it as 'farm' not 'works'). He was known not so much for the prime tomatoes that he grew at work, nor for the very ancient motorcycle on which he pop-popped to and fro, but for the fact that he wore exactly the same clothes, layer after layer, in the depths of winter and height of summer. "What keeps the warmth in'll keep it out" was his philosophy, and I doubt if he had a day's illness in his life.

Precisely where Wendover begins in the London Road – or where it ends in Aylesbury Road – I have never been sure, but for the purpose of this record I intend to begin at *The Halfway House* and end at *The Swan*. This provides an immediate excuse to record that between the wars there were sixteen public houses in Wendover, plus, for half that time, the British Legion Club. Sixteen pubs for a population nowhere near 5,000 seems a remarkable number, and perhaps it is little wonder that at my last personal count, three no longer exist.

All sixteen will be referred to late in their appropriate chapter, but for the impatient and quizzical, they were: *The Halfway House, Leather Bottle, Well Head* (which puzzled me as a boy by advertising itself as a Free House), *King and Queen, Railway Hotel* (or *Shoulder of Mutton*, one of two with an alternative name) *Kings Head, Two Brewers, White Swan, Red Lion, Nags Head, Pack Horse, Rising Sun* (or *Four Seasons*) *Rose and Crown, George, Marquis of Granby* and *Swan*.

The community north of the *Halfway House* comprised the last habitations for a mile or so, well into Wendover, and it was perhaps to achieve some identity that it came to be know as Little London. I can think of no other reason, although the name occurs in other parts of the country.

Wendover's commercial life began here with the Rances – Dan the butcher on the right, Vic the coal merchant on the left – and Goode's garage, destined to become arguably the country's smallest munitions factory in WW2.

Jack King and his wife set up a plumbing business and cafe, respectively, hereabouts in the early thirties.

The next landmark is the gate and drive to Boswells. Not that I have ever used the drive, preferring to approach the house from what is now known as Hogtrough Lane but to us was never more than simply Barkers Lane. It was along that lane that Miss Smith}s class of around twelve-year-olds walked every year for the annual treat of strawberry and cream tea, galloped or strolled around the grounds (dependent upon whether boy or girl) and glimpsed at the collection – mini-museum would be a better description – of the kind that could only be assembled by a physician to the Royal Family as Sir Thomas Barlow was (I believe that Barlows Disease is still on record) and a granddaughter to Charles Darwin, as I believe Lady Barlow was.

Onward along the London Road, to the speed restriction signs and I can just recall the universal resentment that 30mph limits caused. I recall more clearly the introduction of Belisha beacons, named after a Minister of Transport who not long previously had changed his name from Horet Elisha to the Anglicised Hore-Belisha. It was to be some 30 years or more before Wendover gained the first of his brain-children.

Adjacent to the 30mph signs there is now another indication that the visitor is approaching Wendover. In the time of which I write he would have appreciated the fact only by glancing rightwards at the Parish Church and its graveyard. Here are buried my father and mother and some other forebears. Here also, in May 1948, I did one of the most sensible things in my whole life in marrying my Barbara. Here, too, my daughter, Diana, was baptised. I will return to the recollections of the Church of St Mary towards the end of my thoughts.

With Hampden Pond, on the opposite side of Church Lane, I associate dire warnings of the perils of its unknown depths. Certainly I know of no-one foolhardy enough to skate or slide on it (it seemed to be frozen every year when I was a boy) because Hampden Pond was known, or at least reported, to have claimed one or two lives around the beginning of the century. The pond was stocked with fish in the thirties and became the less-than-happy hunting ground of Wendover Fishing Club, which also boasted a boat house and boat. Whether the fish hid in the unknown depths or floated out through the grating at the Heron Path end I doubt if anyone ever knew, but whatever the reason, there was never much to be caught.

Hampden Meadow, next door, was given to the town by Sir Thomas Barlow as a Recreation ground to celebrate the Silver Jubilee in 1935. Prior to that, the majority of Wendover children had to make the long trek to Ashbrook if they sought the pleasure of the swings and seesaws.

The playing equipment, shelter and toilets erected at Hampden Meadow were of a very high order, but they became a prime target for vandals almost from the day the field was opened, and they have remained that way since.

As a youngster I attended one or two services at what was then the Baptist Chapel which carves its corner out of Hampden Meadow. My upbringing in the Church of England made it hard for me to accept that the more free-and-easy atmosphere, the preacher in everyday clothes, the lack of a pulpit and the accoutrements that I took for granted, could constitute a religious ceremony. I was well aware, however, that here were some of the most enthusiastic worshippers, the most ebullient singers of hymns, that I had ever encountered. Is there still that same wholeheartedness, I wonder?

Across Chapel Lane to Witch-hill, to give it what I believe to be its original name, scene of many of my happiest childhood days. Indeed, my first genuine memory is of standing on the raised bank of one of the two Witchell ponds with a bandage covering a knee, cut or grazed in a fall. These ponds were less deep and we were able to shoe-skate and play our form of ice-hockey every winter.

In spring and summer we would net fish in the stream that flowed beside the ponds. How many ghosts of sticklebacks and newts flow beneath the kitchen diners, unobserved by those who now live in what was our beloved Witchell. The field was a great location for trees – tall elms, a couple of walnuts, spanish chestnuts, horse chestnuts among them. Some were victims of storm and lightening between the wars – I remember cows killed in such circumstances - whilst many more trees succumbed later in the whirlwind that spun its way through the town in the early fifties.

If one were to seek a residential area of Wendover that most closely resembles that of the 1930s, Bacombe Lane could stake its claim (along with Ellesborough Road and Perry Street). I recall it in three ages. As a toddler-to-ten year-old, standing on the railway bridge pretending not be frightened as the puff-puff-puff of trains billowed their noisy smoke from one side to the other. As an errand boy heaving the heaviest of fully loaded delivery bicycles every Saturday, perhaps two or three times, the largest load going right to the top of Bacombe Warren (and not realising that the young lady who occasionally refreshed me with a drink and biscuit would many years later become my daughter's Godmother). Thirdly as a walker on my way to Bacombe Hill on one side or through fields and woods to the *Leather Bottle* on the other. (Note to newcomers. Look not now for the *Leather Bottle*. Its last earthy remains were overgrown many a year ago, and more's the pity).

Does latter-day bureaucracy permit the stretch of London Road to the High Street junction to be called South Street? Because South Street it is, just as Ellesborough Road from the railway bridge downwards is Pound Street, Aylesbury Road from the Clock Tower to Wharf Road is Aylesbury Street, and the lower reaches of Hale Road are Paradise. The little bit between High Street and Back Street is Great Lane and Addington Cottages off Aylesbury Road is Frog's Island. No doubt I'll recall more such examples as I ramble on.

These are the names of the past. South Street's *King and Queen* public house for instance, was noted for its Chesham and Brackley Brewery ales, claimed by devotees to be the best beer for many a mile. What happened to the Chesham end I don't know, but Brackley Brewery has long been a Bronnley Soap factory. Sheer sacrilege!

Licensee of the *King and Queen* was a Mr Dupoix. I wouldn't swear to the spelling but would like now to know the derivation of the family name. And, indeed, that ascribed to the eldest son, Diddle Dupoix. We were great ones for nicknames in those days. Gordon Birch was, for some reason, Purdle Birch and since he was virtual leader of his gang the members were Semi-Purdle, Demi-Purdle and so forth. Roy Eggleton was 'Gig' because of his unusual giggle; Roy Wells, 'Bomber' after Bombardier Billy of the same surname; but why Ron Hill was 'Bros', short, presumably for Brothers, I'll never know.

After the Dupoixs at the *King and Queen* came Ted Cockle who, if nothing else, achieved fame for erecting one of the first two television aerials in Wendover and, what's more, not only buying the set to go with it, but installing it in the Lounge Bar for the entertainment of customers. That was the time of an hour or so television a day plus important events like the celebrated Boon versus Danaher fight which in nineteen thirty something attracted a packed audience of drinkers to the *King and Queen*. Yet a purser on the Queen Mary told me, in 1952, that the first question asked by Americans on their way over here was "Do they yet have television in England?" Wendover watched it when the USA had nothing!

Refreshment of a non-alcoholic nature was provided a few doors further on by Mrs Franklin's Lilac Tea Cafe, though I could never quite fathom why a Lilac house should repeatedly be painted orange and black, as it was until and after the last home-made scone and rock-cake was served. Next door – in those days, but not now – was for some time a surgery, or at least that part of the house so dedicated by Doctor Hamilton.

One doorstep further on is Chiltern Lodge, although none of my contemporaries would have recognised the name, so used were we all to calling it the Haunted House. It had at last two claims to fame. In my time it was the home of a reasonably successful author whose son, James Cameron, became far better known, first as the finest journalist (true meaning, writer for daily newspapers) that I have ever read and in more recent years, as a radio and TV personality. Its other claim worthy of note was to have in the garden a magnificent mulberry tree. Not long ago I heard James Cameron reading his autobiography in serialised form on the radio, and he made mention of the tree but did not say whether he fed its leaves to silkworms. I did, and beautiful cocoons they span for me, the fascinating little creatures.

If Ted Cockle's television was a pointer to Wendover of the future, then the shop that is now Deans was a reminder of Wendover past. The shop now is hardly a massive emporium, but it is an enlargement on what I remember was owned by Jack Dean's grandmother. Then less a shop than a barn with a window, it seemed to stock little more than skeins of raffia, hanks of rope and balls of string, all hung from the ceiling. If there were other products they must have been candles, various blackenings, whiteners and polishes and, because most shops of that kind served it, presumably paraffin.

Eventually the old lady became too frail to run what little business there was and her daughter gave up the private kindergarten she had run in Aylesbury Road and moved with her husband and two sons to begin the transition towards the grocer's shop that flourishes today.

Of her two sons, Ron, the elder, was arguably the brightest academician in Wendover of his generation, and the younger, Jack, was undeniably the town's finest whistler. He was later to put all that breath, his willpower and his energy into successfully overcoming the effect of the terrible illness that beset him whilst serving in the RAF.

The shop two doors away what is now a boutique had more humble origins as a dairy. Several times, as it seemed to alternate between private residence and supplier of milk, not really operating as a true dairy as did other establishments that I shall mention in due course.

Completing the north side of South Street was the workshop and office (actually fronting High Street alongside its shop window) of Fred Wood, builder and decorator, whose yard for the store of timber, ladders and sundry building material was further west between the *King and Queen* and the Lilac Cafe. In later years and in Monopoly fashion, Fred was to buy odd pockets of property and land, including the premises in which my father established his business, to give him a sizeable portion of the rectangle bounded by that builder's yard in South Street and the Post Office Yard in High Street. It contains some fascinating gardens and wasteland seen by very few people.

On the western side of South Street there were three properties well worthy of mention. One was a building that served as one of Wendover's private schools during the week and doubled on Sundays as a religious meeting place for some unorthodox religion, the denomination of which I have no idea. Certainly it was close enough to C of E for my parents occasionally to allow my brother to attend Sunday School there along with some of his mates.

Next door was Bert Landon's shop and printing works – a glorified name for two small hand-fed treadle presses and a flatbed poster press that was set with wooden type, a lever-operated guillotine and sundry printers accessories all crammed into the tightest of spaces that somehow still found room for the residue of one of Bert's manifold hobbies.

What can I say of Bert Landon? In his time printer, Oddfellow, parish councillor, cinematographer behind both camera and projector (many's the show he presented in the old Public Hall) collector of cacti and anything else that took his fancy, lighter of fireworks, purveyor of medicaments of the kind one found in corner shops but never chemists and, himself a non-smoker, the unintentional helping hand to would-be schoolboy smokers by dint of a penny-for-three cigarette machine on the outer wall of his shop. Not only three for a penny, either, as the packet contained one Russian, one Turkish and one Virginian. Were those the days! If there is something to be said of Bert it is that I have a photograph of him and my father taken before either was ten years old, In many ways, neither of them ever quite grew up.

As a printer Bert had a debit and credit side to his abilities. To his debit he was guilty of untold literals (the technical term for printers' errors) and he had difficulty meeting promised delivery dates (show me a printer who doesn't). To his credit he provided the intelligent populace with hours of enjoyment looking for those errors, he ensured that every fete and flowershow for miles around was well publicised by posters and he provided in untold quantity the brightly coloured certificate which at those same galas and shows proclaimed First Prize, Second Prize, Third Prize and Highly Commended. I have some which testify to his labours and my luck. Few, if any, of those who now refresh themselves at the Landon Cafe can be aware of the personality of the man after whom it is named.

In the grass-covered corner beyond these tea rooms there once stood

Wheelwrights, Watering Cans and Witchell

Nora Thorne's sweet shop, which holds for my brother and me fond memories of four-ounces-a-penny. The residue of each box and jar would be tipped into one dispenser and sold at what no-one, but no-one, was wealthy enough to call fourpence a pound. Four ounces a penny, for those of us lucky enough or hard-working enough errand-wise to have a Saturday penny. The memories of little Nora go much further, however, for it was our privilege, having the only premises suitable for the ritual of a bonfire to call on her every Saturday with the plea "Any rubbish, Miss Thorne?". At any time of the year the answer was likely to be affirmative and we would have the thrill of a blaze and reward by way of a sweet or two. Bonus time was after Easter and Christmas when our barrow load of rubbish was torn apart in a search for the dummy packs and beautiful three-dimensional showcards that Cadburys and the like supplied to shopkeepers for window display. Could my appreciation of this material have eventually manifested itself when, many years later, I won the Regent Street, London, window display competition? I sometimes wonder.

One last nostalgic glance at South Street reminds me that here would sometimes rest the giant steam engines of Pettigr oves Fair, awaiting its twice-yearly six o'clock emergence on the High Street. More of that later. The engines and their trailers would park beside what is now a garage and in those days was a field in which, as in some other meadows, I am old enough to have memories of the collections and sales of sheep and cattle that were a part of Wendover fair.

Our travels have reached the first crossroads. Pound Street to the left, Dobbins Lane ahead and High Street to the right. It would be customary to turn right, as do the majority of travellers, but in my wanderings it is more logical to turn left, and I will.

Here in Pound Street, from the junction to the railway bridge, we have one of the most photographed and painted parts in Wendover, the attraction of a thatched roof and yellow-painted cottages being what they are for artists and photographers. Of the commerce that can be seen, two shops one hotel and a railway station, I have personally worked part-time at the shops, full-time at the station, and supped many a pint at the pub.

Few would nowadays realise that in the thirties there was another commercial activity in Pound Street in the form of a Model Laundry, as it called itself, beside Lime Tree House. It had moved from Aylesbury Road, lock stock and chug-chug delivery van with, I believe, solid tyres. Solid or pneumatic, they were sufficient to break the leg of Ken Landon who rode carelessly on his red bicycle and became the envy of us all with his leg in plaster and a long spell away from school.

Back down to the grocer's shop for a moment, where the present incumbent has managed to retain much of the original nature of a good old fashioned grocery store. I recall, in the days of Kinghams, the tins of biscuits, glass-topped to display their loose contents; the drawers and metal containers of cereals and spices, teas and coffees; dried fruit and miscellanea, the sacks of sugar, weighed out into blue paper bags, other sacks of I can't remember what, neatly rolled down to reveal their contents; butter patted into shape; rounds of cheeses wire-cut to within a half-ounce of their desired weight. Such goods as were packaged were generally of a higher quality – and anyway more expensive – than those of Wendover's other emporia.

From here every Saturday to the years immediately before the war I would deliver goods, to Worlds End in one direction and Bacombe Warren in the other, with a trip or two up and along Ellesborough Road and the Hale. I did this on an errands boy's bicycle, with a large, deep basket at the front and a sign written (usually by my father) beneath the crossbar. If ever a contraption merited the name 'push bike' it was mine, overloaded with groceries and with a couple of cans of paraffin hanging on the handlebars to prevent me breaking the newly imposed speed limit.

For a full day of this from eight until six I was paid a sum that no matter how measly – and it was, on reflection – was collected in a Silver Jubilee money box (1935 vintage, courtesy of Oxo) and from there withdrawn to contribute a little something to the cost of clothing a growing lad.

On Easter, Whit and August Mondays, I would take my talents next door to the baker's shop of Harry Thompson, which on these bank holidays became supplier of ice cream, and my task was to trundle, by truck or errand boy bicycle, large chunks of ice from Charlie Spittles' fishmonger.

For this I was paid about the same amount as for the many hours of Saturday toil next door, and this money I was allowed to spend on Easter Eggs or at the fete, depending upon the Monday in question.

Right through to the end of World War II, Thompson's bread was delivered to outlying districts by pony and trap. Harry, like many bakers of his day, had a profitable sideline in the best-fed pigs and chickens for miles around.

The *Shoulder of Mutton* was favoured between the Wars by a certain strata of men that I could not describe without use of the word 'class', and of that I have no intention. Instead I will say that they appeared to favour Wethereds beer available nowhere else (expect perhaps the *Well Head*) and more probably they favoured membership of the Wendover Bowls Club which in those days had a very good green behind the *Mutton*. The club house was a hut sufficiently spacious enough to be used occasionally, as an alternative to the Public Hall, for the entertainment of children at concerts given by conjurers, ventriloquists and music makers, and for seasonal parties. That hut was also the headquarters of the Home Guard during the war, and was sometimes used for annual dinners of sports and other clubs but was eventually and unfortunately destroyed by fire.

The adjacent railway station must inevitably find a place in my narrative. My father's sister reputedly died as the direct result of a cold caught whilst watching the opening ceremony in eighteen-ninety something. My father vied with Percy Parsons and the Carter brothers for taxi trade between the wars – it was not so much that inhabitants of Wendover and its surrounds had money to spend on taxis as that they had no alternative means of transport.

As for me, my very first gainful employment was at Wendover Station in 1940 in its halcyon days of servicemen's travel, on posting and leave. The period is, however, outside that of my self-imposed brief and I will say only that the line was officially designated Metropolitan and Great Central Joint Committee which meant that London Transport and the London and North Eastern Railway alternated responsibilities for various activities on a five-year cycle, and I was always proud to be an LNER appointee, although eventually engaged by LT.

The route through Wendover was the last main line to be built in Britain, and it had expresses starting at Marylebone and calling at Harrow, Aylesbury, Rugby, Leicester, Loughborough, Nottingham, Sheffield and Manchester.

The Master Cutler ran this way, as did some fine old LNER engines named after football clubs. Train spotting at Wendover could be a fascinating hobby and one on which my brother was keen.

In its early days, Wendover station was the terminal point for the Rothschilds of Halton and Tring, and for visitors to Chequers. It was also the point of arrival for the enthusiastic, bright-eyed lads who came to sit the RAF apprentices entrance exam at Halton, and the departure point for the unfortunate failures who went home sad-eyed and dejected.

Those who stayed would at leave-times, twice yearly perhaps, be marched down to special trains at the station at around six in the morning, headed by a pipe band. I developed then a love of bagpipes that has stayed with me all my life.

POSTSCRIPT

Here the recollections of Oliver finish. He began writing on 1 February 1978 and he died on 2 September 1979. His ashes are buried in St Mary's churchyard. In his "beloved" Witchell is planted a whitebeam tree, which has for these past 20 years been growing to his memory.

Diana Arnold

Nee Floyd

Chapter 22

The Lone Ranger

And now it's my turn. Compared with all that precedes, my memories seem insignificant, but as this book will be around when I am long gone, I hope my descendants will be able to glean something from the social history. As for the moment, maybe some of my old friends will read it and remember with affection our schooldays in the fifties and sixties.

I was born at 31 High Street, the house Harry recalls as being occupied by Mr H G Landon. It is now 'Lazy Daisy' – a needlecraft shop. I remember it as two shops: Hamilton's jewellers on the right and Godwin's newsagent on the left, where I worked on Saturdays during my teens. Other shops recalled by Harry are the grocers on the corner of Dobbins Lane owned by Mr F. W. Blake and the bakers shop owned by Harry Thompson (Oliver recalls both these too). In my childhood the grocers was owned and run by the family of my friend, Frances Dunnett. It is now an off licence. The baker's, in my day called The Anne Boleyn and now a restaurant called Le Bistro, was run by two sisters, one of whom was called Winnie. She had a habit of "straightening" pictures hanging on the wall and to this day when we see a lopsided picture we say that Winnie has been there!

Harry also recalls the *Kings Head* yard, site of the Hollands Brewery up to the time of the Great War. The *Kings Head Hotel* was demolished in the early 1960s to make way for the shops, car park and library that now stand on the whole site. The nearby path, next to which grew a hazel tree supplying very tasty nuts, used to be known as Brackley Path and led to Witchell fields. Witchell ponds (so lovingly remembered by Oliver) were drained and given over to the Witchell housing development at the same time. I spent many a Saturday night in one of those houses, babysitting for the Ballantine family.

Just up the rise from the *King's Head*, Harry speaks of the draper's shop kept by a Mr Edwin King and his daughters. This shop was, until very recently, still a draper's and in my time called 'Bells', 'Edwards and Dobsons' and then 'Biddies'. It has now been converted into two shops. I shopped in 'Bells' for some sewing accoutrements. I had seen on Blue Peter how to make a sewing box and wanted to buy some needles, but was astounded at what I thought was the cost of them marked on the packet. What I had failed to realise was that the price was in fact the size of the needles!

The parade of shops on the other side of the High Street, on Manor

Wheelwrights, Watering Cans and Witchell

Waste, that Harry refers to as being kept by old Mr Freeman, still stands. In my childhood it was three shops. On the right was a television repair shop owned by somebody I knew as Alex (Mr E. Jankowski). He had grown his little finger nail very long – could he *really* have used it as a screwdriver?

In the middle was a restaurant, "The Friar Tuck", owned by Mr and Mrs Eric Niblett. I had many a delicious meal there, washed down by 'Hubbly Bubbly' which was variously flavoured fizzy fruit drinks in dimpled glass bottles. On the right was a chemist shop owned by Mr Douglas Sargeant, where my mother was employed as a dispenser. The restaurant and chemist's were eventually made into one large chemist's and the other shop rents videos. From the age of about eight I lived in the property behind these shops. Although it has been converted into a dental practice the outside still looks the same and the name plate 'Twin Wells' is still on the door. The garden has disappeared and is now a car park.

Carter's Garage, next door, was demolished in the 1960s and a supermarket and newsagent now occupy the site. The concrete floor of the old garage is mentioned by Harry as having been part of monasterial buildings associated with Bosworth House (number 27 High Street). Hibberd's Garage was also demolished in the 1960s and the site given over to building development off Back Street. The shop Harry knew as Essex and Son I remember becoming 'International Stores' in the 1960s and is now a Chinese restaurant.

Just around the corner in Aylesbury Street Harry refers to the 'present fire Station'. At the time of his memoirs this was by the side of the Parish Rooms, about 100 yards along on the left from the clock tower. It was demolished later and two cottages built in its place, one called 'Fyre'.

The only thing I remember of my baby years was my doll – a boy doll named Aloyisious. My real first memories are of Hampden Road, where I lived at number 27. I can still recall in my mind's eye the view down over Wendover and especially the fairs in May and October with the coloured lights shining and hearing the music from the roundabout, if the wind was in the right direction. The name on the canopy of the galloping horses was Pettigrove and all the horses had their names painted on the neck. For those children who weren't daring enough to sit on one of the horses, they could sit in a dragon with nostrils flaring – the dragon not the children! Oh, the memory of the toffee apples; candy floss was off the menu – too sugary! There were lots of other sideshows – penny arcade, hook-a-duck, roll-the-ball, swingboats, coconut shy – positioned on the Manor Waste and up Pound Street.

Back to Hampden Road. We had a couple of cars that I remember – one that had a windscreen that could be wound open – and that had to happen on a couple of occasions when the pea-soupers of the fifties made it extremely difficult to see! The number plate of that car is fixed firmly in my brain: HMN 986. A later car was a Squire, with wood strips down the bodywork, which my friends and I would 'drive' in our make-believe games. The streets were safe in those days, and as Hampden Road was a cul-de-sac not much traffic would disturb our street games. Games that have never even been heard of, let alone played, by today's electronic games-loving children such as 'Farmer, farmer may I cross your golden river?, 'What's the time Mr Wolf?', 'The farmer's in his den'.

Although I am an only child I was lucky enough to be surrounded by families with children. On one side lived 'Uncle' Ken and 'Auntie' Yvonne Thomas with their children, Joanne, Stuart, Andrew, Keiran (and the baby whose name I can't recall), and on the other side were 'Auntie' Connie and 'Uncle' Alan Tickner with their daughter Jacqueline. Of course the adults were not really aunties and uncles, but it was not the done thing in those days to address adults by just their first names.

My first friend was Stephen Simmonds who was the son of my mother's best friend (and bridesmaid, whose name was also Barbara). They lived in Clay Lane and as babies we were pushed out together in our prams and later pushchairs . One of our favourite outings was to the station cafe. There we would have Vimto; the name still recalls to me the smell of steam engines! On Thursday afternoons (early-closing day) Mum would take me to see my Godmother, Cicely Webb who was housekeeper to the Tetley family at Bacombe Warren. On fine spring days we would go into the surrounding woods with Effan, the Tetley's corgi, and admire the bluebells, cowslips and primroses which abounded. The sound of a startled blackbird still evokes for me Bacombe Warren where we would have tea in the large, cosy kitchen. A bell, in the stairwell of the house, looked to my child's imagination like a face with its two large eyes; I was so scared to go upstairs thinking the face was going to get me!

One of the photographs shows me astride a horse, being held very tightly by my father! The photograph was taken at a fete where the guest of honour was Davy Crockett! I don't actually remember the fete (I must have blocked it from my memory) but I have been told that I screamed extremely loudly when confronted by Mr Crockett – it must have been the tail hanging at the back of his head!

I started at Wendover Church of England School in the autumn of 1958 and was very disappointed when told that I couldn't wear the watch I had been given for my fifth birthday. The members of staff whose names come

96

Wheelwrights, Watering Cans and Witchell

readily to mind are Miss Mavor, Mrs Armstrong, Mr Hearn, Miss Jones (mentioned in Wilf's part!) Mrs Airey and Miss Hindle. Mrs Armstrong was a small lady who sat on a high chair and looked down on us little ones with a stern look on her face. Mr Hearn taught in a temporary classroom in the infants' playground. This classroom was overhung by a horse chestnut tree grown from a conker planted in the 1930s by my father when a pupil at the school.

Miss Jones was still teaching in the early 1960s and it is her I have to thank for getting me through the eleven plus. When I was at the school from 1959 to 1963, she taught the oldest children in one of the top classes. When I reached that class, her reputation had gone before her, but I respected her and worked hard for her. I was one of four children in her class in my year to pass the eleven plus and go on to secondary schools in Aylesbury. More children in the other top class, taught by Mr Pammenter (who went on to become Headmaster after the retirement of the Reverend Figg Edginton) also passed. Mrs Airey and Miss Hindle used the huts away from the main part of the school and I can remember learning how to do joined up writing (I had such trouble with 's', they used to look like bananas) and long multiplication. I also learned some lovely poetry in those classrooms and entered into the poetry competition in the end of year Speech Day. In 1962 I won the Junior Verse Speaking Prize with *Puppy and I* by A. A. Milne and had the honour of standing on the stage in the Memorial Hall in Wharf Road and reciting it to the assembled parents. The prizes given at Speech Day were books, and I still have the two books I won (the other was a Progress Prize). The one for the poetry was the Good Housekeeping Children's Cookery Book and even now, I still refer to it!

One year I was the female lead in the Christmas school play and spent most of it tying up the cord around my dressing gown. I forget the name of the play but the slippery cord became, I am told, the highlight of the show!

The headmaster of the School during my time there was the formidable figure of the Reverend Figg Edgington. I was very in awe of him, he was an imposing figure in his flowing, black cloak and dog collar. His assemblies are etched deeply in my memory; I learned many of my favourite hymns there (I can still sing our school hymn *He Who Would Valiant Be* off by heart) and also gained a love of classical music. At the end of each assembly he would play us a piece of music and we would sit quietly and listen. Two that I particularly remember are *The Poet and Peasant Overture* and some of the pieces from *Peter and the Wolf*. The piece that portrayed Peter himself was used as the signature tune to a popular television programme of the time, and when the music started you could hear the whispered words '*Zoo Time*' gently echoing round the hall. It being a church school we often used

97

to walk along the Heron Path to St Mary's Church for services and when I was in the choir (goodness knows how I managed that feat with my voice) I would sit in the choir stalls and sing the descant to the Crimond tune to the 23rd Psalm, *The Lord Is My Shepherd*. I still get butterflies in my stomach when I hear that tune. Ascension Day was a highlight for us for we would all go to church for a service and then have the rest of the day off.

One of my favourite lessons was spent in the open air, usually in Witchell, studying the flora. The class was divided into small groups and each group studied one particular section of flora or fauna. I especially remember sitting on a fallen log in Witchell studying grasses and being delighted to discover the lovely names of each species. One of the prizes given at Speech Day was the Botany Prize and I have pressed many a wild flower to be stuck into a scrapbook in the hope of winning. I never did. My least favourite lesson was PE, as I once fell from a form which had been placed at an angle against the hall wall and jarred my back – although I always enjoyed country dancing, and can still to this day 'Strip the Willow'!

Friends at school included (in no particular order) Zoe Didsbury, whose father had been in the services and they had lived abroad before coming to Wendover; Frances Dunnett, whose family owned the grocer's shop on the corner of Dobbins Lane; Pauline Slade whose father was the manager of the Co-Op store in Aylesbury Road and who used to regularly beat me at tennis; Frankie Escott who lived with her family on the outskirts of Wendover towards Weston Turville; Jonathan How lived in Hale Road. He was the one who denied me the honour of being the baby born nearest to the date of the Queen's coronation, by eight days! Other school friends (some of their surnames elude me) were: Roger Adams, Nigel Gillett, John Condy, Robert Nugent, Susan and Marilyn Diston (twins), Diana Milroy (the vicar's daughter), Gary Stamper and his sister whose nickname was Bambi, Nicholas Chamblett, Jenny and Sally (I was given a pair of china poodles which I named after these two and was distraught when one was knocked on the floor and smashed), Jenny Petrons (who I believe later married another school friend, Peter Keates), Elizabeth, whose mother was a chiropodist, Robert Bramble, Luciana Passaro, Patsy Rich, Michael Foster and another set of twins, Angela and Brenda Tyrell. I used to have one of those long school photographs which unfortunately has mysteriously disappeared, but if I had it I am sure I could bring some more people to mind.

During the long cold winter of 1963 Hampden Pond, the pond between the church and the rec., froze over and a group of us found a dead pigeon, gently placed it in a shoe box and pushed it across the ice to where there was a hole in the middle and thus buried it. It was a very solemn occasion.

Wheelwrights, Watering Cans and Witchell

For some reason (possibly Christmas parties) the school used to have fancy dress competitions and I remember two of my costumes. One was as a parcel. Dad made strategically placed holes for my legs and head in a very large box and covered it with paper. The luggage tag announced that the parcel was destined for Lady Ina Fod (an anagram of Diana Floyd). Another competition took place at the time of the first telecommunications satellite launch and I went as Telstar. I wore a net tutu and on my head was a creation made from a sort of crown with a balloon in it. In the crown were tiny bulbs which were attached to a bell push hidden in my hand. As I walked around I pushed the button and the lights flashed. I'm not sure if I won either of the competitions, but the ingenuity of the costumes is down to imagination and flair on my parents' part.

Sports Days at the school were held in the rec. and I can recall many a sack, bean-bag, skipping and obstacle race (not my favourite). We all belonged to different 'houses' which were commonly known by their colours: Red, Blue and Yellow, although they had names: blue, my house, was Coombe. The other two were Bacombe and Hampden, but which way round?

In 1963 I passed the eleven plus and left the relative comfort of the village school to go to what was then the Aylesbury Technical High School (and is now the Sir Henry Floyd School – no relation) and made a whole lot of new friends, but I recall my first six years of education with much pleasure.

I spent a lot of my play time away from Wendover school in the back garden of 27 Hampden Road. I had a paddling pool, the water in which always had to be treated with gentian violet – polio was rearing its ugly head in the 50s. There was also a swing, a wigwam and a big, old trunk, the latter two of which were used in our make-believe games. Children's imaginations in the 50s and 60s were, I am convinced much livelier than now. We sailed many an ocean blue in our trunk 'ship' and visited many a foreign land wearing our dressing-up clothes!

My birthday parties took place in June and they always seemed to be in the back garden, summers must have been warmer then. One of my favourite party games was finding dried peas! A packet of such peas was sprinkled all over the garden and guests were each given a receptacle and a time limit to find as many peas as they could: the winner was the one with the most! Such simple pleasures!

My pet during the days at Hampden Road was a budgerigar, or to be precise, two budgerigars, called Chico. There were two because the first one took advantage of an open window to fly to his freedom! The second one was bought to console me, so he had to be called Chico as well.

When I was three I started ballet classes and they continued until my feet grew too large (and the rest of me too, I suspect) and the wrong shape for pointe ballet shoes. I took part in many shows, as rabbits and pixies, etc., and took examinations in Natural Movement and Ballet. One of the dances I recall I was dressed as Little Miss Muffet and another was to the song *I had a Little Nut Tree*. The ballet classes were held in the mirrored room behind the chemist's shop; the school belonged to Mr and Mrs Sargeant and was run by their daughters 'Miss' Yvette and 'Miss' Daphne. Their other daughter, Wendy, had a son, Guy, who went on to be a principal at the Royal Ballet. Miss Yvette also taught Sarah Brightman in the other Sargeant School of Dancing in Hemel Hempstead.

One of the pleasures of summer was walking up to the monument and back. Those of us brave enough and fit enough, scrambled down the escarpment towards Butlers Cross and then climbed all the way up again before taking the more gentle way down back to Wendover. One winter I went tobogganing on part of the hill, but it was not a pastime I repeated because a lad who was also there had, I thought, the good manners to let me go first and then proceeded to follow immediately and bump into me and knock me off. That's probably why I have never felt the urge to do any winter sports.

One of the joys of childhood was belonging to the Guides first as a Brownie and then a Girl Guide and finally, although not for long, a Ranger. The Brownies met in the hall of John Colet School and I was a Gnome, gaining my Sixer's stripes before flying up to Guides. Every summer the Brownies of the district met and held 'Revels': a glorified picnic with games and songs. One year our pack went dressed as Robin Hood and his Merry Men. I went as Will Scarlett in one of Dad's shirts dyed bright red.

The Guides met first in the Literary Institute and then in the new Guide Hut in Manor Road. I also became patrol leader in Guides and helped out as a pack leader in the Brownies assuming the name of Squirrel. When I was too old to be a Guide I became the only Ranger (The Lone Ranger!) in Wendover. There were no others wishing to join me however, and rather than join a group in Aylesbury I gave up guiding for good.

Wendover Guides used to collect old newspapers; probably the beginning of recycling. My photograph was taken and a report written in the local paper, but how I collected it with a wheelbarrow one bad winter, possibly 1963? I remember walking on top of the deep, snow, and not breaking the icy top. To gain one of my badges for Guides I undertook to do the shopping for the ladies and gentlemen in the newly opened old people's

Wheelwrights, Watering Cans and Witchell

warden-controlled flats at the end of Clay Lane. I continued to do it long after I had my badge. I took a number of other badges which have set me up for a life of domestic bliss – Cook, Child Care, Laundress!

Mum worked at Sergeant's chemist shop dispensing medicines during my school days and so I used to go to Nana's for my lunches. It was just a short walk up High Street to number 29 where she lived. The cottage consisted then of one entrance passage/hall, a small living room, small pantry, scullery and three bedrooms upstairs. There was no bathroom or inside toilet. As two cottages, prior to 1888, the living space must have been minimal. The back garden was a patch of lawn and some outbuildings: the outside toilet and two workshops, which were full of old instruments and tools. I never ventured into these workshops, there were too many cobwebs for my liking. However I used the brick walls for innumerable games of 'two ball' which involved bouncing two tennis balls against the walls, catching them and chanting rhymes. One started "Nebuchadnezzar the king of the Jews, Bought his wife a pair of shoes". How it continued escapes me, but I know the game involved a lot of bouncing of balls over arm, under arm, under leg and body twirling. Another game I played by myself with the aid of two chairs and a length of elastic was "French Skipping". This involved jumping over and twisting around in and out of the elastic which was stretched tight between the chair legs. If there had been two other people the elastic would have gone around their ankles, then knees and then thighs.

Back to Nana's lunches; how I remember those delicious lunches! We had the same meal on the same day each week:

Monday:– cold luncheon meat with a red casing that had to be stripped off.

Tuesday:– mince or rissoles made from the left over Sunday roast.

Wednesday:– yellow fish, which I disliked eating for a long while because a loose tooth fell out while I was eating it once and I blamed the fish!

Thursday:– stew: such succulent meat and vegetables

Friday:– white fish, probably plaice, gently steamed in milk

Sometimes the whole family would all go to Nana's for lunch on a Saturday: steak pie with the most light delicious suet pastry ever tasted.

After lunch, when I was small, Nana would read 'The Robin Family' in *Women's Weekly* to me, and then close her eyes for 'forty winks'. During holidays I would stay at Nana's all day and one of my favourite games was to cut clothes and shoes from a catalogue and have a 'shop' neatly laid out on the flap of the large bureau that used to live in her front room. There wasn't a lot of room to move in that front room: there was the bureau; a round table and four chairs; two easy chairs and a sideboard on top of which sat the little black and white television (BBC only). There wasn't much scope for changing the furniture around either because of the lovely coal fire that always seemed to be burning during the cold winter months. My heart skips a beat now when I think that one of my pleasures was burning brightly coloured spills in the fire!

Another of my pastimes at Nana's was surveying the traffic driving along the High Street. I used to divide a sheet of paper into columns and write down the colours of the cars and when one passed I would put a mark against the relevant colour. I can't imagine doing that these days: so many cars with so many different colours!

One of my less favourite memories is of visits to the dentist – Mr Inman – a large man who always seemed to want me to open my mouth wider! Immunisations against childhood ailments were also not very pleasant, but the thought of my reward of sixpence to buy a Jamboree Bag or a bar of chocolate helped me through the pain! I bought these treasures at the sweetshop next to *The George* public house. The other shop where I spent my pocket money was Jeals in Hampden Road. They used to sell many things, including coloured pencils and I remember wanting to buy some just before one Christmas and being denied. How did my parents know that Father Christmas was bringing me some? My other memory of Jeals shop is being stung by a bee and someone cutting an onion in half to put on the sting. It must have worked because I remember the smell of the onion more than the pain of the sting.

How I wish I had as fantastic a memory and wonderful way with words as Grandad Harry, Uncle Wilf and Dad because I'm sure I could have written more, but I have come to an unwilling halt. I hope you have enjoyed reading these memories of four members of three different generations of the same family as much as I have enjoyed compiling them.

I left Wendover temporarily in the summer of 1969 at the age of 16, when I left school, and moved with my parents to a new detached house in Brackley, Northamptonshire. However, I moved back a couple of months later to live with my grandmother at the family cottage, 29 High Street, when I gained a place at Slough College of Further Education and needed digs. I stayed with her for another couple of years until I finally left and moved back to Brackley. Eighteen months later, in 1972, I married Mike Arnold, whom I had met in Banbury Oxfordshire, so not all good things come from Buckinghamshire, and three years later gave birth to Gavin.

At the time of writing Mike and I live in Reading, but my heart still belongs to Wendover and always will.

Appendix 1

The Floyds of Buckinghamshire

The following was written by Wilf, following extensive research during the 1970s and 1980s and adapted slightly by Diana after more research.

There is an overgrown grassy track in the village of Lacey Green, near Princes Risborough, named Kiln Lane. There's little sign of habitation at the end of the lane but time was, it's fair to assume that the Floyds hailed from very near here. I say this because in the church records of baptisms, marriages and deaths the term 'Kiln man' occurs around 1800, with an earlier reference of 1703 describing a John Floyd as a brickmaker.

Records for Joseph and John Floyd, brothers baptised in 1794 and 1793 indicate that they married sisters Jane and Sarah Tyler. The records for the baptisms of Joseph's children show that he was at one time a kiln man. It seems that Joseph possibly died of smallpox at the age of 59 in 1852 and was buried at 10pm. A William Floyd who was buried at the age of 76 in 1822 was also described as a kiln man. Other trades referred to are 'Labourer' (circa 1640), with Yeoman and Farmer featuring into the middle nineteenth century. Two things are certainly clear from the family history. The first is that the Floyds were a well-established clan in Lacey Green at least as far back as the middle 1500s and the second is that they were of fairly humble stock. They were also god-fearing I imagine, if church record entries are any indication.

What about the name itself? Dictionaries of surname origins tend to vary about Floyd, giving Flower, Flud or Lloyd as some derivatives. I turn again to the parish records where, in the sixteenth century, entries are spelt Fflyde or Fflydo; later it became Ffloyde before setting down to the current usage. My belief is that the name came from Flud, Anglo-Saxon for 'by water', as this tends to line up with the village life and trades mentioned.

What took me to Lacey Green in the search for origins? First instincts were to go to Tingewick in North Bucks, in the knowledge that great grandfather William had farmed there in the mid 1800s, but I found little there or in the General Record Office to link with that area. What I did have though was the memory of my uncle Jack Floyd who linked William with a Miss Hawes of Lacey Green, and it was a short step from there to trace the marriage certificate in the GRO (although peculiarly this showed that the wedding took place at Uxbridge parish church.) Nevertheless, the records showed a pattern of entries in the High Wycombe area around that period so

I was pretty well convinced that that was where a search should start.

The GRO records are very interesting in themselves. Fortunately the quarterly registers which date from 1837 contained only about a dozen Floyds each quarter so the task was not difficult. The pattern of registration showed that London, Truro and Birmingham were other centres of the clan, and it would be interesting sometime to establish whether a common link existed somewhere in the distant past. Some entries in the records can also be misleading to anyone not sure of connections. For example, there is an entry recording the death in the Towcester district in December 1839 of a certain Oliver Floyd. The fact that my brother Oliver died in Towcester in September 1979 is a sheer coincidence and completely unrelated, although a neutral researcher could be forgiven for assuming a link.

Census records from 1821 supplement the GRO records and list the household of Joseph Floyd, William's father, in Lacey Green. More details about the census later, but it was possible to work back from the point into the parish records.

The church records of Princes Risborough (including Lacey Green) date from 1562 and are held in the Aylesbury archives. Some of the earlier writings are difficult to decipher and because of the gaps the linking of various generations is very much a matter of interpretation. However it was possible to construct a direct line dating back to Joseph and Eleanor Floyd who were born around 1690.

Novelty of first names was not a very strong feature in those days and recurring family names complicate the direct line construction. Joseph, William and John recur frequently; John and William were two sons of Jeffrey Fflyde who married in 1570 and the names recur over the next ten generations. Joseph comes into the picture around 1700 although it could be earlier; the church records are indistinct. I believe it was not unknown for names to occur twice in the same family when, for example, the first born died young and the name was given to a later child.

There are a few examples of break-away from traditional names, such as the children of a Joseph Floyd (labourer and nurseryman), girls called Rosina, Maria and Rose-Maria. Common names for females in the district seem to have been Sarah, Elizabeth and Mary.

What's in a name?

So far as my own family's direct line is concerned, first names showed a break-away from the Lacey Green tradition in the late 1800s when grandfather Joseph married into the Rayner family. His children's names

Wheelwrights, Watering Cans and Witchell

were Alice Lavinia (died young) and Harry Thomas (my father) and were of Rayner origin. The break continued when he named his daughter Alice Elizabeth (Rayner names), one son Oliver Reginald Thompson (the first two names after army friends and the third his wife's maiden name) and the other son Wilfred Joseph (the first from another friend and the second a return to Floyd traditions). Oliver's daughter Diana, and my son Michael have names chosen solely by family preference with no connections at all, and Michael will, if the occasion arises, have to decide whether to restore traditional names to his offspring. Grandfather Joseph, who was widowed fairly young, had a son by second marriage into the Eldridge family, whose name, John William Francis, had Eldridge and Floyd connections.

Of course, with the smaller families of today there is not the scope for name spreading. Great-grandfather William was one of six children and he himself had twelve children. Most of them farmed around north Bucks or married farmers in the area (Byfield, Woodford Halse, Preston Capes). Their various children continued farming in the same area. The Tingewick branch is still going – William's great-grandson Robert, lives in Buckingham with his wife Su and their daughter, Harriet.

Since the branch of our family settled in Wendover, contact with other branches tended to be few and far between. However, before this record starts to concentrate on Wendover let's return for a while to the Lacey Green of great-great-grandfather Joseph Floyd and his forebears.

Lacey Green

Although the village trades were humble the Floyds did however appear to have been property owners over the years. In the baptism record for 1576 is a certain Cyleb, Gyles, or Giles Floyd (difficult to read). His will is in the Aylesbury archives and although difficult to read in its entirety the following extracts give an idea of the life and times. It also tends to show the way that lawyers of the day could make their money by over-embellishment!

In the name of God Amen ... the six and twentieth day of April in the year of our Lord one thousand six hundred and forty Gyles Floyd of Lacey Green in the parish of Princes Risborough in the county of Bucks, Labourer, being sound and firm in body but of whole mind and in good ... My last will and testament in the manner and form following ... My soul into the hands of God my maker hoping of life everlasting ... And of my body to be buried in decent manner at ... Goods to my friends hereinafter names, and my worldly goods to Anne my wife the cottage and commons wherein I now dwell ... to Anne my wife ... of her natural life ... I give and bequeath to Richard Ffloyd the youngest sonne of my brother Thomas Floid the said cottage... And if it

shall happen that the said Richard Floid to dye before Anne my wife ... my
will it ... the said cottage and common shall ... to the ... of my brother
Thomas Floyd. I will my ... in my chamber two ... cupboards and a table and
from in the hall one Craffe and a craffe bottle ... to my brother William Floyd
and to Mary his daughter five pounds.

It appears that Gyles and his wife were childless, but who actually got
the cottage is a bit obscure. The baptism records show the names of Gyles
(1576), William (1580), and Thomas (1584), their father being John Fflyde,
born I imagine around 1550 before the records started. The first identified
direct line ancestor in my constructed tree is Joseph Floyd who was born
sometime towards the end of the 18th century. He was married in 1710 to
Eleanor/Ellinor Free and had five children His will was written in 1745 and
executed in 1758, two years after his death:

In the name of God Amen Joseph Floyd of Lacey Green in the parish of
Princes Risborough in the county of Bucks, Brickmaker, being of sound and
perfect mind and disposing memory thanks be given to Almighty God, do
make and ordain this my last will and testament in manner and form
following that is to say first I give my soul into the hands of almighty God
trusting through the death and passion of Jesus Christ my saviour and
redeemer to inherit everlasting life and my body I commit to be decently
buried at the discretion of my executors hereinafter named and on touching
temporal estate whereso with it both pleased Almighty God to bless my with
I give and bequeath as followeth Item. I give and bequeath unto my loving
wife Eleanor Floyd all my freehold cottage with yards, gardens, barns
backsides and orchards with all my ways waters commons profits
commodations and appertanances belonging to the same and which are
being at Loosely Row and Princes Risborough and also all my freehold
lands lying and being within the parish fields and bounds of Princes
Risborough aforesaid with this and every appertanance belonging to in any
way appertaining all which said lands and premises I give my same loving
wife during the term of her natural life and after the decease of my loving
wife then my will and meaning is that my said lands cottages (etc) shall
descend and be to the user and behest of my son William Floyd to him his
heirs and assigns for ever and also I give and bequest unto my loving wife
Ellinor Floyd all my copyheld cottage in Princes Risborough aforesaid
withn the yards, barns, gardens, backsides, waywaters, common profits,
belonging to the same, and also my copyheld lands lying and being within
the parish fields and boundaries of Princes Risborough aforesaid which
cottages lands I give and bequeath to my said loving wife to her and her
heirs for ever. Item. All my goods and chattels and arrears of rent and all my
personal estate whatsoever and wheresoever I give and bequeath to my

Wheelwrights, Watering Cans and Witchell

loving wife Ellinor Floyd who I make ordain and appoint my full and sole executrix of this my last will and testament. In witness whereof I have to this my last will and testament set my had and seal the eleventh day of May in the year of our Lord one thousand seven hundred and forty five. Joseph Floyd subscribed published and declared by the testator to be his last will and testament.

There was a codicil to the Will:

On June 8th 1758 the goods of the late Joseph Floyd late of Princes Risborough decd according to the last will and testament was granted to William Floyd the natural and lawful son of Ellinor Floyd widow and sole executrix names in the said will dying before she had taken upon her the execution of the said will.

From the family tree it is conjectured that although Joseph had three other children, Joseph, John and Mary, William was the only unmarried one at the time of the codicil and therefore was the inheritor. William married a girl called Elizabeth and had six children, three of whom died in infancy: Elizabeth aged two and twin daughters Elizabeth and Eleanor. His other children William, John and Mary all lived into adulthood and it is John who continues our line of succession.

John married Sarah James in 1792 and had four children. Their first child, John, died in his first year. Joseph, born in 1794, married Jane Tyler in 1820 while his brother John (a very popular family name that seems to be meant to be carried on!) married her sister Sarah in 1823. Our interest is in Joseph who was the father of William Floyd (later of Tingewick).

What was Lacey Green like at the time of Joseph and Jane? For this I turn to the census records for 1821. There were 33 houses in the village, housing 40 families and the population totalled 196 with 102 males and 94 females. By deduction therefore the average family was just under five people, although in each house there was an average of six occupants. The trade of the wage earners was mainly agricultural (34) but seven were described as 'trade'.

The age dispersal of the population was as follows:

	Male	Female
Under 5	19	24
5 - 10	17	10
10 - 15	9	6
15 - 20	13	7
20 - 30	19	15

107

	Male	Female
30 - 40	10	14
40 - 50	8	6
50 - 60	2	6
60 - 70	3	5
70 - 80	1	1

In Joseph Floyd's house there were five people, three males with one under five and two between 20 and 30, and two females, one aged 15-20 and the other 50-60. The under five would be John, the other male Joseph's brother John and the elderly female probably their mother Sarah. Joseph was in trade at the time, while John was in agriculture.

At the next census in 1831 Joseph was described as a shopkeeper. John had married and left and widow Sarah had died, but there were still five in the house. Jane had had two more children, William now aged six and Eliza, four. The village population had risen by 35% to 267 with 140 females and 127 males, the female numbers having risen twice as fast as the males. There were also 15 more houses during the ten year span.

By the time of the 1841 census, the family of Joseph and Jane had increased by three: Emma, now nine, Dan aged six and Sarah-Jane two. Joseph's brother John had, by this time, it seems, set up home at Speen and had four children: Mary, Peter, Jacob and George and we will leave that branch of the family there. In all probability their descendants are still around that area. William by this time was aged 15 and described as a shoemaker in the census. In 1847 he married Sophia Hawes. She could not read or write (the marriage certificate bore an X) but there was nothing exceptional about this at the time. Sometime in the 1850s they left Lacey Green for Tingewick and we will leave Lacey Green too, at this point, briefly following William to Tingewick but then moving with his son Joseph (my grandfather) to Wendover.

William Floyd (1824 - 1900)

As previously mentioned, William was shoemaker at the age of 15 and he was still in this trade when he married Sophia in 1847. His father Joseph was a grocer at this time. Exactly when William went to Tingewick is not known but it was sometime in the 1850s. His first son Joseph (my grandfather) was born in 1852 and although he may have gone with the family to Tingewick he certainly moved back to Princes Risborough later in life.

William and Sophia had twelve children in all, most of them at Tingewick. Apart from Joseph, who was fourth to be born, they were:

Lucinda: born before her parents marriage, no children.

Julia Emma: Married Thomas Walker.

Cora: married George Perkins.

John: lived at Preston Bissett. One son.

Thomas: farmed at Preston Capes. Married twice, no known children.

Frederick: nothing known, possibly went to America.

Daniel: lived at Woodford Lodge, Eydon. Died single.

Emma: married James Tack, farmer, lived at Byfield. No children.

Hannah Dinah (known as Nancy): died single.

Ada: married Johnathan Nicholls, lived at Goddington.

Children: Cyril, Donald and Ellen (known as Lulu).

Frank: farmed at Tingewick with family.

Children: Percy, Cecil, Lily and Gladys.

It will be seen from this list that the direct line is very thin, with Joseph and Frank having the only male descendants (John's son having died single). As previously mentioned Frank's son Percy also farmed at Tingewick and had a son Robert. Joseph's line of course includes yours truly!

William and Sophia are buried in Tingewick cemetery having died in 1900 and 1908 respectively.

Joseph Floyd (1852 - 1935)

Although the writings of Harry Thomas Floyd go into some detail of life with his father, there is not much about Joseph's earlier life. Indeed, it's all a bit obscure, although it's apparent that he put his hand to a number of things. He was presumably brought up at Tingewick but farming, it would seem, did not appeal to him. According to Jack Floyd he went to the USA on a windjammer to seek work, but returned after a short while. The first authentic mention after that is Harry Floyd's recall that he was inn-keeper of 'The Bell' at Princes Risborough, at the same time as he was carrying on a wheelwright's trade on the premises. Nearby competition then caused him to up sticks and head for Wendover.

He was of quite striking appearance in his younger days as evidenced by his photo, but I remember him as a kindly white haired and whiskered old man, approaching 80 at the time.

His first marriage, to Elizabeth Rayner, ended in 1909 when she died at the age of 48, and he subsequently married Annie Eldridge. Elizabeth was apparently unwell a lot of the time which presumably accounts for the fact that son Harry spent much of his childhood with Rayner grandparents at Kimble while father Joseph concentrated on his trade.

Joseph lived at the premises at 29 High Street Wendover until his second marriage when he moved to 'Hill View', 129 Aylesbury Road in Wendover. Regarding the business, I can recall him firing the iron hoops for cart wheels, and also adding to the thick layers of paint on the paint shop door when testing colour mix. A large hoarding at the top of the yard announced Joseph Floyd and Son, because Harry went into the business when of age, before enlistment for the First World War. Joseph, meanwhile, had a son John William (Jack) by his second marriage and devoted the necessary time to his upbringing. They also adopted a girl Margaret (Maggie) who later became a very kindly aunt to Harry's children. She married Jim Climer and lives in Aylesbury.

Joseph died peacefully in bed at the age of 83 and is buried, together with his two wives, in Wendover churchyard.

Appendix 2

Births, Deaths and Marriages

Extract from parish records - Baptisms

1.2.1562	Henry Fflyde was baptised
25.4.1566	Isabel Fflyde was baptised
12.4.1569	John Fflyde was baptised
9.3.1571	William Fflyde was baptised
30.9.1572	Annye Fflyde was baptised
21.2.1574	Elynor Fflyde was baptised
1.10.1576	Cyleb Fflyde was baptised
17.12.1578	John Fflyde was baptised
17.12.1578	Elizabeth Fflyde was baptised
12.7.1580	William, the sonne of John Fflyde was baptised
21.9.1581	John, the sonne Fflyde was baptised
10.2.1584	Thomas the sonne Fflyde was baptised
16.2.1585	William the sonne of Fflyde was baptised

The rest of this book was difficult to read and was left for later study

5.7.1723	Mary, daughter of Joseph and Eleanor Floyd
29.7.1739	John son of John and Sarah Floyd
15.5.1743	Joseph son of Joseph Floyd and Mary his wife
29.7.1744	Thomas son of John Floyd and Sarah his wife
20.12.1747	Mary daughter of Joseph Floyd and Mary his wife
17.1.1747	Joseph son of John Floyd and Hannah his wife
31.7.1748	Sarah daughter of John Floyd and Sarah his wife
1.4.1749	John son of William Floyd and Elizabeth his wife
21.5.1749	Mary daughter of Joseph and Mary Floyd
27.5.1751	Elizabeth daughter of William and Elizabeth Floyd
2.8.1752	Caelia daughter of Joseph and Mary Floyd
22.2.1754	Elizabeth and Eleanor twins of William Floyd and Eliza his wife
27.10.1754	Thomas son of Joseph and Mary Floyd
6.3.1757	Joshua son of Joseph and Mary Floyd
23.4.1757	Mary daughter of William and Eliza Floyd
12.8.1759	Joshua son of Joseph and Mary Floyd
22.6.1760	Elizabeth daughter of John Floyd and Elizabeth his wife
10.1.1762	Hester daughter of Joseph and Mary Floyd
7.10.1764	Thomas son of John Floyd and Elizabeth his wife
6.1.1766	William son of Joseph Floyd and Sarah his wife
12.8.1770	John son of John and Elizabeth Floyd
12.5.1781	Joshua son of Joshua and Sarah Floyd
15.7.1787	William son of Joshua and Sarah Floyd
27.3.1791	Joseph son of William and Mary Floyd
22.3.1793	John son of John and Sarah Floyd
9.12.1793	James son of William and Mary Floyd
8.1.1794	Joseph son of John and Sarah Floyd

5.1.1796	Elizabeth daughter of John and Sarah Floyd
22.6.1800	George son of William and Mary Floyd
8.5.1803	Thomas son of William and Mary Floyd
21.1.1820	John son of Joseph (Kilnman Lacey Green) and Jane Floyd
4.7.1824	William son of Joseph (Yeoman late of Lacey Green and of Meadle) and Jane
4.7.1824	Mary daughter of John (Yeoman Lacey Green) and Sarah Floyd
5.9.1824	Rosina daughter of Joseph (Labourer of Culverton) and Mary Floyd
6.8.1826	Caroline daughter of Joseph (Husbandry labourer of the town) and Mary Floyd
16.9.1827	Eliza daughter of Joseph (farmer of Meadle) and Jane Floyd
6.4.1827	Maria daughter of Joseph (Husbandry labourer of the town) and Mary Floyd
11.4.1830	Thomas son of Joseph (labourer of the town) and Mary Floyd
10.4.1831	Peter Tyler son of John (labourer of Speen) and Sarah Floyd
22.4.1831	James son of Joseph (Labourer of P Risborough) and Mary Floyd
17.6.1832	Emma daughter of Joseph (Shopkeeper of Lacey Green) and Jane Floyd
4.2.1834	George son of Joseph (Labourer in husbandry of P Risborough) and Mary Floyd
25.12.1835	Dan son of Joseph (Shopkeeper of Lacey Green) and Jane Floyd
5.6.1835	Rose Maria daughter of Joseph (Labourer in husbandry of P Risborough) and Mary Floyd
7.8.1836	Jacob son of John (Shopkeeper Lacey Green and Sarah Floyd
1.12.1839	John son of Joseph (Labourer of P Risborough) and Mary Floyd
14.4.1840	George Tyler son of John (Shopkeeper Lacey Green) and Sarah Floyd
7.6.1840	Sarah-Jane daughter of Joseph (Shopkeeper of Lacey Green) and Jane Floyd
17.3.1843	Frances daughter of Joseph (Nurseryman of P Risborough) and Mary Floyd
7.10.1843	Jane daughter of John (Shopkeeper Lacey Green) and Mary Floyd

Extracts from Parish Records - Burials

12.1.1571	Joan Fflyde
17.5.1580	Thomas Fllyde
5.6.1585?	Fflydo
26.12.1609J	John Ffloyde
25.12.1653	Thomas Floyde
3.5.1684	Eliza daughter of Jo: Ffloyd was buried
17.3.1685	Ruth Ffloid of Lacey Green was buried
30.5.1685	Anne Flloyde: yr daughter of John Ffloyd was buried
21.12.1697	Anne Ffloyd was buried
1.2.1703	John Ffloyd a brickmaker was buried
2.9.1713	Jos son of Jos Ffloyd was buryed
15.7.1726	Mary daughter of Joseph Floyd
26.2.1754	An infant of William Floyd and Eliza his wife
9.12.1756	Joseph Floyd
16.2.1757	John Floyd

20.5.1757	The widow Floyd
18.8.1758	A child of Joseph Floyd
25.11.1764	A child of John Floyd
5.4.1766	Joseph Floyd
29.7.1767	Mary, wife of John Floyd
17.12.1767	Joseph Floyde
9.1.1768	John Floyde – a poor old man
20.9.1770	A child of John Floyde
12.10.1783	John Floyd
13.3.1785	Joseph Floyd
28.2.1786	The wife of William Floyd
20.4.1786	A daughter of Joseph Floyd
17.11.1786	The widow Floyd
19.11.1789	The wife of Joshua Floyd
23.5.1793	A child of John Floyd
15.8.1794	The widow Floyd from Pen
15.6.1797	A child of William Floyd
13.7.1800	John Floyd
23.6.1801	William Floyd of Lacey Green (Yeoman)
17.8.1810	Eliza, wife of William of Floyd of Lacey Green - aged 62
23.10.1810	Mary, widow of Joseph Floyd of Lacey Green
25.4.1811	George, son of William and Mary Floyd (Labr) Aged 11
30.12.1811	Thomas Floyd (Bachr) late of Lacey Green - son of John (insane)
30.7.1820	Joshua Floyd, late a soldier in the 14th Regt a foot age 37
31.10.1822	William Floyd widow, Kilnman Lacey Green Age 76
26.1.1834	Maria – daughter of Joseph and Mary - Risboro Age 7
3.2.1834	Rose – daughter of Joseph and Mary - Risboro Age 101/2
24.1.1837	Keziah – widow of William Floyd - Risboro Age 70
7.1.1839	Sarah Floyd Loosely Row - Age 77
5.5.1840	Mary Floyd, wife of William Floyd, Culverton, Age 74
24.4.1840	George Tyler, son of John and Sarah Floyd, Lacey Green Age 9 mths
28.5.1840	Jacob, son of John and Sarah Floyd Age 4yrs
3.7.1843	Mary, daughter of John and Sarah Floyd, Lacey Green Age 19yrs
2.8.1843	Sarah, wife of John Floyd, Lacey Green, Age 40

About this time Lacey Green began its own parish records

24.3.1845	William Floyd of town Age 79
11.1.1852	Joseph Floyd of Town Age 59 (died of small pox, buried at 10pm)
26.1.1855	Joseph Floyd of town – infant
25.10.1861	Ruth Floyd Little Kimble Age 31

Extracts for Parish Record - Marriages

(Note: An S against the name indicates a signature in the register, i.e. literate; an M indicates a mark in the register, i.e. illiterate

11.7.1567	Thomas Fflyde and Joan (?) Hoarner
24.11.1570	Jeffery Fflyde and Joan Bryan

Record barely legible later until :

12.1639	William Fflyde and Jane Bristow

Parish books 3 and 4 (1685 to 1754) no Floyd entry spotted in quick examination, although in view of the baptism records of parent this is probably my omission, not the records.

12.11.1764	Joseph Floyd (S) and Sarah Lee (M)
23.12.1769	Thomas Floyde (S) and Sarah Hearn (S)
9.4.1782	Joshua Floyd (M) and Sarah Lipscombe (M)
31.1.1788	William Floyd (M) and Mary West (M)
10.7.1788	William Floyd (S) and Eliza Hone (S)
13.11.1792	John Floyd (S) and Sarah James (S)
24.2.1793	Joshua Floyd (M) and Mary Cleydon (M)
21.4.1797	William Floyd of Saunderton (M) and Keziah Edwards (M)
7.9.1820	Joseph Floyd of Lacey Green (S) and Jane Tyler of Loosely Row (M)
31.3.1823	John Floyd of Lacey Green (S) and Sarah Tyler (S)

No further entries spotted pre 1837. Subsequent records are in the GRO.

Extracts for 1841 Census returns

Census Area	Names	Age	Occupation
Church Street, Princes Risborough	Mary Floyd		
	Caroline		
	Thomas		
Culverton, Princes Risborough	William Floyd	76	Agricultural Labourer
Lacy Green	Joseph Floyd	45	Agricultural Labourer
	Jane	40	
	John	20	
	William	15	Shoemaker
	Eliza	14	
	Emma	9	
	Dan	5	
	Sarah	2	
Lacey Green	John Floyd	40	Agricultural Labourer
	Sarah	35	
	Ann	13	
	Peter	10	
	John	7	

114